Teacher's Edition

Jason Renshaw

Tara Cameron

Series Editors: Cecilia Petersen and Mayumi Tabuchi

Published by
Pearson Longman Asia ELT
20/F Cornwall House
Taikoo Place
979 King's Road
Quarry Bay
Hong Kong

fax: +852 2856 9578
email: pearsonlongman@pearsoned.com.hk
www.longman.com

and Associated Companies throughout the world.

First published 2007
Reprinted 2007

Produced by Pearson Education Asia Limited, Hong Kong
EPC/02

ISBN-13: 978-962-00-5903-2
ISBN-10: 962-00-5903-4

Publisher: Simon Campbell
Senior Editor: Howard Cheung
Project Editor: Jessica Balde
Designers: Junko Funaki, Tonic Ng
Illustrator: Balic Choy
Audio Production: David Pope and Sky Productions

For permission to use copyrighted images, we would like to thank © Bob Rowan; Progressive Image/Corbis (pp. 4 RT and 10 T), © Robbie Jack/Corbis (pp. 4 RC and 10 C), © B. Bird/zefa/Corbis (pp. 4 RB and 10 B), © H. Schmid/zefa/Corbis (p. 18 L), © Martyn Goddard/Corbis (p. 18 R), © Brynner Victoria/Corbis Sygma (pp. 5 B and 20), © NASA Jet Propulsion Laboratory (pp. 23, 24 B and 34), © Steve Lee (University of Colorado); Jim Bell (Cornell University); Mike Wolff (Space Science Institute); NASA (p. 24 T), © 1989 Roger Ressmeyer/NASA/Corbis (p. 24 C), © The International Astronomical Union/Martin Kornmesser (p. 29) © Dr. R. Albrecht, ESA/ESO Space Telescope European Coordinating Facility; NASA (p. 30), © Larry Williams/Corbis (p. 37 Bkgd), © George Shelley/Corbis (p. 37 T), Chris Stowers © Dorling Kindersley (p. 43 Bkgd), © Atlantide Phototravel/Corbis (p. 44 T, C), © Daniel Lavabre (p. 48 T, B), © Douglas Kirkland/Corbis (p. 51 C), © S. Carmona/Corbis (p. 52 T), © Duomo/Corbis (p. 52 B), © Ilya Pitalev/ITAR-TASS/Corbis (pp. 57 and 58 B), © Vitaly Belousov/ITAR-TASS/Corbis (p. 58 T), © Troy Wayrynen/NewSport/Corbis (p. 60), © Connie Ricca/Corbis (p. 71 R Bkgd), © Simon Marcus/Corbis (p. 71 L), © LWA-Stephen Welstead/Corbis (p. 79), © Envision/Corbis (p. 86 TT, CC, BT, BB), © Y.Bagros/photocuisine/Corbis (p. 86 TC, BC), © J.Riou/photocuisine/Corbis (p. 86 TB), © Paul Anton/zefa/Corbis (p. 86 CT) and © Lew Robertson/Corbis (p. 86 CB).

Acknowledgements
These reading books are dedicated to my beloved wife, Yeona. Without her patience, support and encouragement, the Boost! series would not have been possible for me to write. Thank you also to the Korean teachers at Jasaeng JS English in Changwon, South Korea, who have been my partners in finding better ways to teach reading skills to young and teenage learners.
Jason Renshaw

The Publishers would also like to thank the following teachers for their suggestions and comments on this course: Tara Cameron, Rosanne Cerello, Nancy Chan, Chang Li Ping, Joy Chao, Jessie Chen, Josephine Chen, Chiang Ying-hsueh, Claire Cho, Cindy Chuang, Linda Chuang, Chueh Shiu-wen, Mark de Boer, Mieko Hayashida, Diana Ho, Lulu Hsu, Eunice Jung, Hye Ri Kim, Jake Kimball, Josie Lai, Carol Lee, Elaine Lee, Melody Lee, Peggy Li, Esther Lim, Moon Jeong Lim, Jasmin Lin, Martin Lin, Catherine Littlehale Oki, Linda Liu, Tammy Liu, Goldie Luk, Ma Li-ling, Chizuko Matsushita, Geordie McGarty, Yasuyo Mito, Eunice Izumi Miyashita, Mari Nakamura, Yannick O'Neill, Coco Pan, Hannah Park, Karen Peng, Zanne Schultz, Kaj Schwermer, Mi Yeon Shin, Giant Shu, Dean Stafford, Hyunju Suh, Tan Yung-hui, Devon Thagard, John and Charlie van Goch, Annie Wang, Wang Shu-ling, Wu Lien-chun, Sabrina Wu, Yeh Shihfen, Tom Yeh, Laura Yoshida and Yunji Yun.

The publisher's policy is to use **paper manufactured from sustainable forests**

Welcome to

Boost! Reading 3

The **Boost!** Skills Series is the definitive and comprehensive four-level series of skills books for junior EFL learners. The series has been developed around age-appropriate, cross-curricular topics that develop students' critical thinking and examination techniques. It follows an integrated skills approach with each of the skills brought together at the end of each unit.

The twelve core units in **Boost! Reading 3** follow a clear and transparent structure to make teaching and learning easy and fun. The reading skills build and progress across the four levels of **Boost! Reading** and are correlated to the next generation of tests of English.

You will find the following in **Boost! Reading 3**:

- Age-appropriate and cross-curricular content-based passages
- A wide variety of text types (academic readings, reports, emails, newspaper articles, etc.)
- Units paired by theme, with a review unit for each pair

Unit Topic

Each unit has a cross-curricular and age-appropriate topic.

Students will

- find the topic directly relates to their own lives and study.
- be engaged and motivated to learn.

World of Magic

Unit 1

A What tricks do magicians do? Discuss your answers.

Reading Skill

Finding the stated main idea

Main ideas can be found at the start, in the middle or at the end of paragraphs. When a main idea is written out in the paragraph, it is called a stated main idea.

B Underline the stated main idea. Then check [✓] where in the paragraph it is.

One of the tricks a magician does is called production. To do this, he produces something from nothing. Examples include pulling a rabbit out of an empty hat, filling an empty bucket with coins or even the magician himself appearing in a puff of smoke.

start
middle
end

9

It's magic!

Magicians perform magic tricks to show that something impossible has happened. There are many kinds of magic tricks.

One kind of magic trick is called production. To do this, a magician produces something from nothing. Examples include pulling a rabbit out of an empty hat, filling an empty bucket with coins or even the magician himself appearing in a puff of smoke.

A magician is holding a coin. He might snap his fingers and the coin suddenly disappears. This trick is an example of the vanish, which is the opposite of production. The vanish is a kind of magic trick in which things disappear. After putting a bird in a cage and then covering the cage with cloth, the magician waves his wand and pulls away the cloth. The bird has vanished.

Perhaps a rope is cut in half with a knife. The magician does something special and suddenly the rope is one complete piece again. Or after tearing a newspaper into pieces, the magician rubs the pieces together and the newspaper becomes whole again. These tricks restore things to the way they were before. Restoration is another common type of magic trick.

Reading

A graded, content-based reading passage, with supporting audio, sets up the main skill practice.

Students will

- find the reading passage stimulating with topics geared to their age level.
- be exposed to a variety of text types—from academic to real-world passages.
- be able to answer comprehension questions to aid understanding.

Reading Skill

A very simple introduction of the targeted unit skill is followed by a skill discovery activity.

Students will

- be introduced to the reading skill in a clear and understandable way.
- discover the reading skill for themselves without the need for long explanations.

Audio CD

The CD at the back of the Student Book provides audio support for all reading passages plus the audio for the Integration listening tasks.

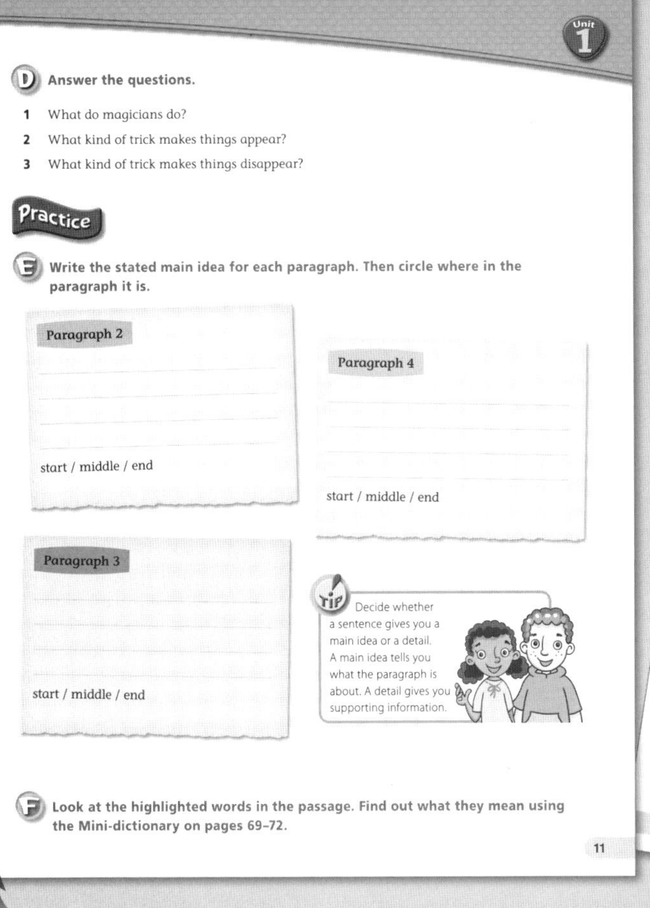

Unit 1

D Answer the questions.

1 What do magicians do?
2 What kind of trick makes things appear?
3 What kind of trick makes things disappear?

Practice

E Write the stated main idea for each paragraph. Then circle where in the paragraph it is.

Paragraph 2
start / middle / end

Paragraph 4
start / middle / end

Paragraph 3
start / middle / end

TIP Decide whether a sentence gives you a main idea or a detail. A main idea tells you what the paragraph is about. A detail gives you supporting information.

F Look at the highlighted words in the passage. Find out what they mean using the Mini-dictionary on pages 69–72.

11

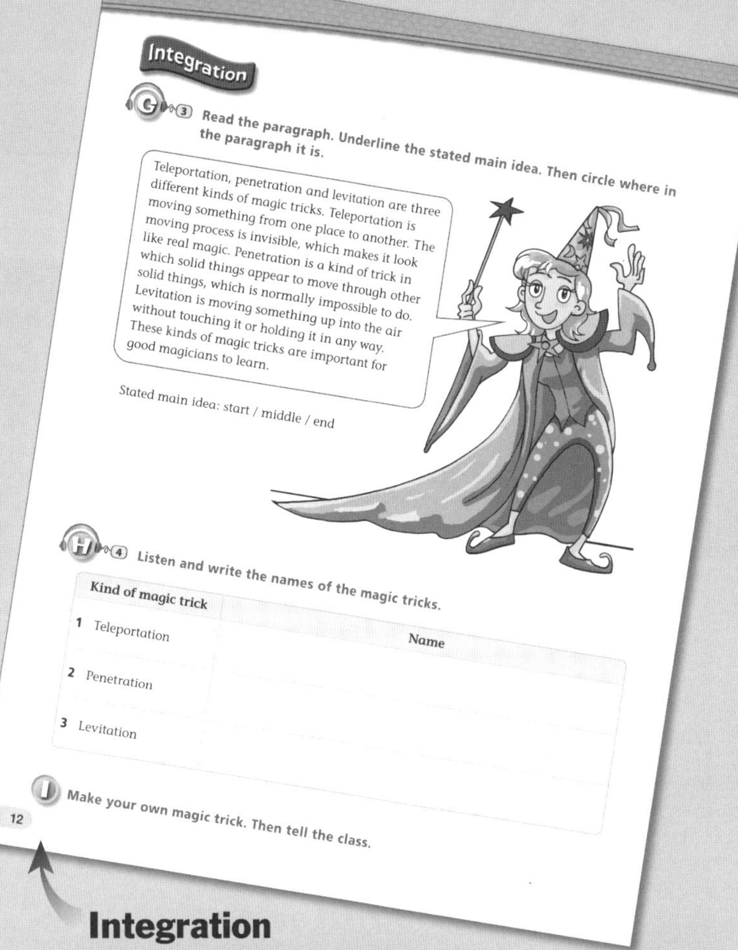

Integration

G 3 Read the paragraph. Underline the stated main idea. Then circle where in the paragraph it is.

Teleportation, penetration and levitation are three different kinds of magic tricks. Teleportation is moving something from one place to another. The moving process is invisible, which makes it look like real magic. Penetration is a kind of trick in which solid things appear to move through other solid things, which is normally impossible to do. Levitation is moving something up into the air without touching it or holding it in any way. These kinds of magic tricks are important for good magicians to learn.

Stated main idea: start / middle / end

H 4 Listen and write the names of the magic tricks.

Kind of magic trick	Name
1 Teleportation	
2 Penetration	
3 Levitation	

I Make your own magic trick. Then tell the class.

12

Practice

A skill practice task is followed by an independent vocabulary-building activity using the Mini-dictionary.

Students will

- be able to apply the reading skill to the passage through meaningful practice.
- develop their vocabulary by learning words in context.

Integration

The reading skill is combined with listening, writing or speaking tasks.

Students will

- learn to use a reading passage to springboard into productive activities.
- develop the language skills needed for the next generation of integrated tests of English.

Review

After every two core units there is a review which consolidates the reading skills already studied.

Students will

- be able to see their progress in using reading skills.
- learn to apply different reading skills to the same passage.

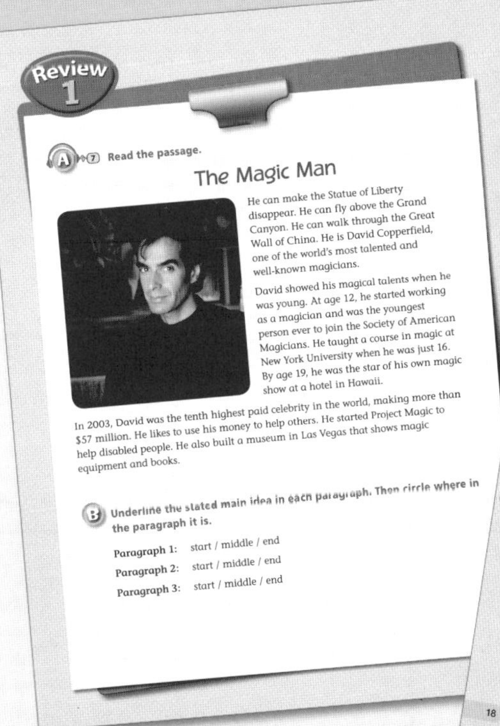

Review 1

A 7 Read the passage.

The Magic Man

He can make the Statue of Liberty disappear. He can fly above the Grand Canyon. He can walk through the Great Wall of China. He is David Copperfield, one of the world's most talented and well-known magicians.

David showed his magical talents when he was young. At age 12, he started working as a magician and was the youngest person ever to join the Society of American Magicians. He taught a course in magic at New York University when he was just 16. By age 19, he was the star of his own magic show at a hotel in Hawaii.

In 2003, David was the tenth highest paid celebrity in the world, making more than $57 million. He likes to use his money to help others. He started Project Magic to help disabled people. He also built a museum in Las Vegas that shows magic equipment and books.

B Underline the stated main idea in each paragraph. Then circle where in the paragraph it is.

Paragraph 1: start / middle / end
Paragraph 2: start / middle / end
Paragraph 3: start / middle / end

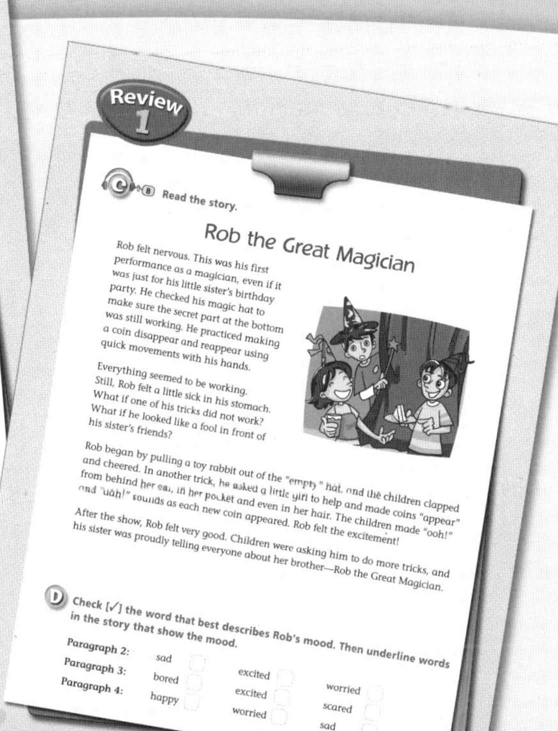

Review 1

C 8 Read the story.

Rob the Great Magician

Rob felt nervous. This was his first performance as a magician, even if it was just for his little sister's birthday party. He checked his magic hat to make sure the secret part at the bottom was still working. He practiced making a coin disappear and reappear using quick movements with his hands.

Everything seemed to be working. Still, Rob felt a little sick in his stomach. What if one of his tricks did not work? What if he looked like a fool in front of his sister's friends?

Rob began by pulling a toy rabbit out of the "empty" hat, and the children clapped and cheered. In another trick, he asked a little girl to help and made coins "appear" from behind her ear, in her pocket and even in her hair. The children made "ooh!" and "aah!" sounds as each new coin appeared. Rob felt the excitement!

After the show, Rob felt very good. Children were asking him to do more tricks, and his sister was proudly telling everyone about her brother—Rob the Great Magician.

D Check [✓] the word that best describes Rob's mood. Then underline words in the story that show the mood.

Paragraph 2: sad / excited / worried
Paragraph 3: bored / excited / scared
Paragraph 4: happy / worried / sad

18

Contents

Unit 1 World of Magic

Unit Overview

SUBJECT	Art and Literature
READING SKILL	Finding the stated main idea
TEXT TYPE	Content-based passage

Reading Skill

Finding the stated main idea

The main idea is the most important idea in a paragraph; it tells you what the paragraph is about. It can be found at the start, in the middle or at the end of a paragraph. A main idea that is written out is called a stated main idea.

Show students a paragraph containing a stated main idea. Have them identify the details in the paragraph and discuss what the paragraph is about. Then have them read out what they think is the most important sentence in the paragraph—that is usually the stated main idea.

A good activity is to have each student write their own paragraph on a sheet of paper, stating the main idea. Then have them pass their papers around for other students to pick out the stated main idea. Keep passing them around until all students have read them.

Answers for Unit 1 Worksheet (p. 13)

Paragraph 1

Harry Houdini is said to be the world's greatest magician ever. (end)

Paragraph 2

He was famous for many tricks. (middle)

Paragraph 3

After a spectacular tour of Europe, Houdini returned to the United States in 1904, where he became a great success. (start)

World of Magic

Unit 1

A What tricks do magicians do? Discuss your answers.

Reading Skill

Finding the stated main idea

Main ideas can be found at the start, in the middle or at the end of paragraphs. When a main idea is written out in the paragraph, it is called a stated main idea.

B **Underline the stated main idea. Then check [✓] where in the paragraph it is.**

One of the tricks a magician does is called production. To do this, he produces something from nothing. Examples include pulling a rabbit out of an empty hat, filling an empty bucket with coins or even the magician himself appearing in a puff of smoke.

start [✓]
middle [ ]
end [ ]

9

2 Read the passage.

It's magic!

Magicians perform magic tricks to show that something impossible has happened. There are many kinds of magic tricks.

One kind of magic trick is called production. To do this, a magician produces something from nothing. Examples include pulling a rabbit out of an empty hat, filling an empty bucket with coins or even the magician himself appearing in a puff of smoke.

A magician is holding a coin. He might snap his fingers and the coin suddenly disappears. This trick is an example of the vanish, which is the opposite of production. The vanish is a kind of magic trick in which things disappear. After putting a bird in a cage and then covering the cage with cloth, the magician waves his wand and pulls away the cloth. The bird has vanished.

Perhaps a rope is cut in half with a knife. The magician does something special and suddenly the rope is one complete piece again. Or after tearing a newspaper into pieces, the magician rubs the pieces together and the newspaper becomes whole again. These tricks restore things to the way they were before. Restoration is another common type of magic trick.

D Answer the questions.

1 What do magicians do? Magicians perform magic tricks to show something impossible has happened.

2 What kind of trick makes things appear? Production.

3 What kind of trick makes things disappear? The vanish.

Practice

E Write the stated main idea for each paragraph. Then circle where in the paragraph it is.

Paragraph 2

One magic trick is called production.

start / middle / end

Paragraph 4

Restoration is another common type of magic trick.

start / middle / end

Paragraph 3

The vanish is a kind of trick where things disappear.

start / middle / end

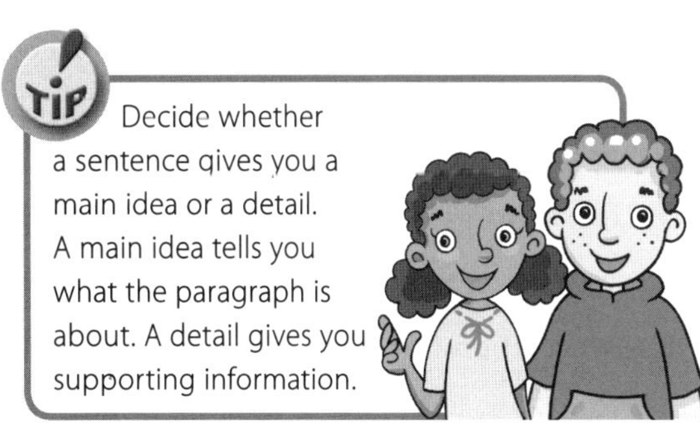

TIP Decide whether a sentence gives you a main idea or a detail. A main idea tells you what the paragraph is about. A detail gives you supporting information.

F Look at the highlighted words in the passage. Find out what they mean using the Mini-dictionary on pages 69–72.

Integration

G 3 **Read the paragraph. Underline the stated main idea. Then circle where in the paragraph it is.**

Teleportation, penetration and levitation are three different kinds of magic tricks. Teleportation is moving something from one place to another. The moving process is invisible, which makes it look like real magic. Penetration is a kind of trick in which solid things appear to move through other solid things, which is normally impossible to do. Levitation is moving something up into the air without touching it or holding it in any way. These kinds of magic tricks are important for good magicians to learn.

Stated main idea: (start) / middle / end

H 4 **Listen and write the names of the magic tricks.**

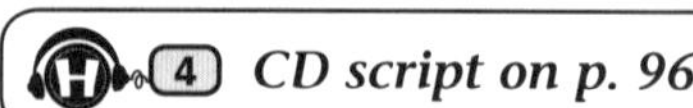

Kind of magic trick	Name
1 Teleportation	The Great Cage Swap
2 Penetration	Through the Card
3 Levitation	Ladyfloat

I **Make your own magic trick. Then tell the class.**

12

Name: ______________________ Class: ______________ Date: ______________

The Great Houdini

Magician Harry Houdini was born in Hungary in 1874. His family moved to the United States when he was a young child. His real name was Erich Weiss, but he changed his name to Harry Houdini when he became a magician. Houdini started off as a regular card magician but later became a master magician in illusions and escape acts. Many of his tricks are still a mystery to this day. Houdini is said to be the world's greatest magician ever.

Houdini escaped from jails, handcuffs, chains, ropes and straitjackets in front of the audience. He was famous for many tricks. One of his most famous tricks was when he made an elephant and its trainer disappear from the stage in the London Hippodrome.

After a spectacular tour of Europe, Houdini returned to the United States in 1904, where he became a great success. In 1912, he performed his most famous act, in which he was upside down in a glass box full of water. He held his breath for over three minutes.

Houdini's last performance was in Detroit in October 1926. He died a few days later at the age of 52.

Write the stated main idea for each paragraph. Then circle where in the paragraph it is.

Paragraph 1

____

____

start / middle / end

Paragraph 2

____

____

start / middle / end

Paragraph 3

____

____

start / middle / end

Unit 2 Show Time

Unit Overview

SUBJECT	Art and Literature
READING SKILL	Identifying moods
TEXT TYPE	Story

Reading Skill

Identifying moods

Mood is the atmosphere or feeling in a situation. Things you can see, hear or feel create the mood. Writers create moods in their stories by giving detailed descriptions. They show mood by their choice of words. The mood from sentence to sentence can change easily depending on the words that are used.

Show students how the mood of the following sentences change with the words. You can then have students write simple descriptive sentences and get them to change the adjectives to see how the moods change.

The angry man in the dark, dirty clothes looked at me.
The smiling man in the bright, clean clothes looked at me.

Even words that have a similar meaning can create different moods. For example, ask students which word creates a stronger mood, *hate* or *dislike*? Then have students list other pairs of verbs or adjectives that they know have a similar meaning. Have them discuss which words create the stronger moods.

Answers for Unit 2 Worksheet (p. 19)

1. I was really upset and started crying.
2. I did not know what to do.
3. I turned around and saw her smiling at me.
4. With each new trick something more amazing happened.

[Suggested answers; students' answers can vary]

Show Time

Unit 2

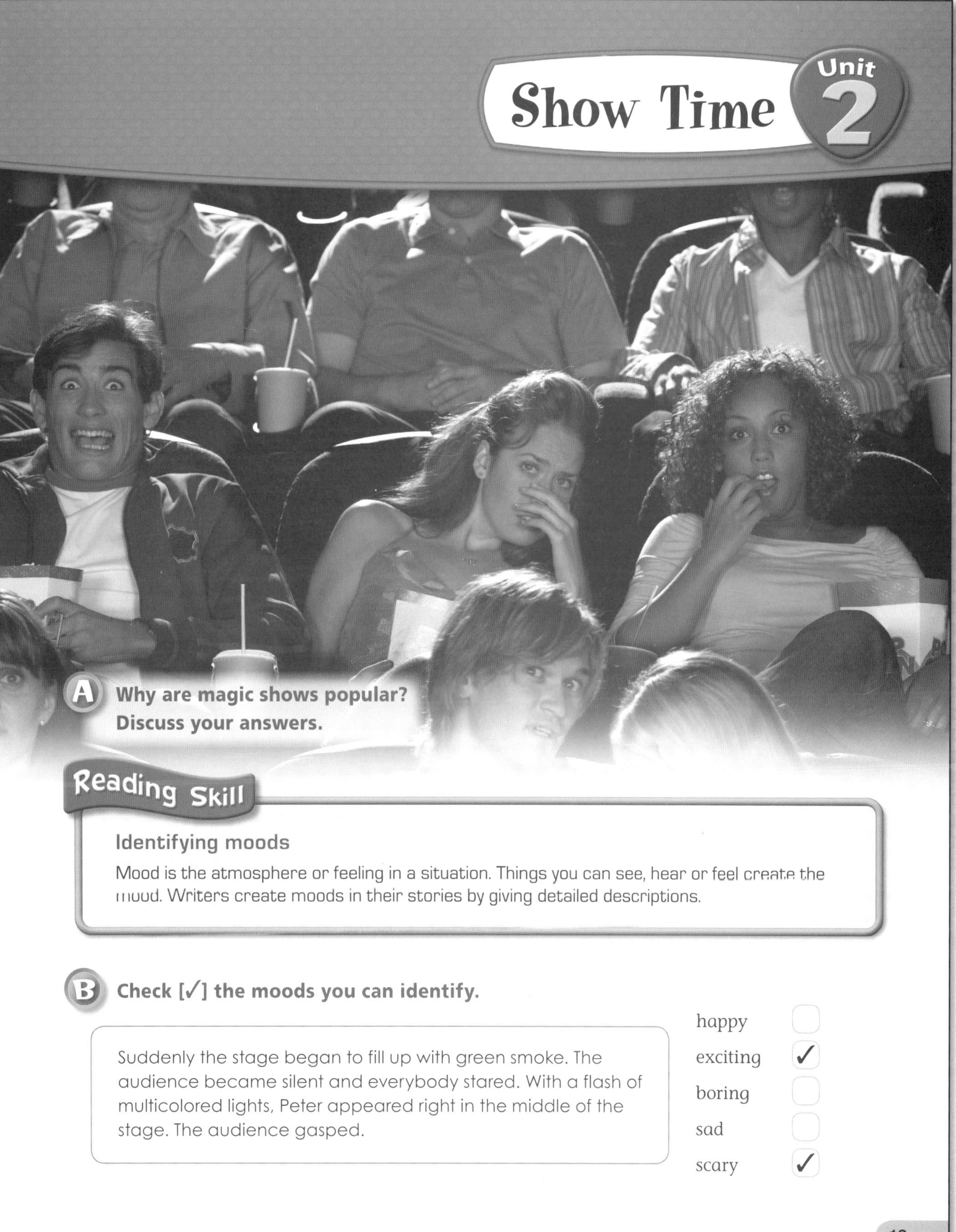

A **Why are magic shows popular? Discuss your answers.**

Reading Skill

Identifying moods

Mood is the atmosphere or feeling in a situation. Things you can see, hear or feel create the mood. Writers create moods in their stories by giving detailed descriptions.

B **Check [✓] the moods you can identify.**

Suddenly the stage began to fill up with green smoke. The audience became silent and everybody stared. With a flash of multicolored lights, Peter appeared right in the middle of the stage. The audience gasped.

- happy [ ]
- exciting [✓]
- boring [ ]
- sad [ ]
- scary [✓]

Read the story.

The Amazing Peter Twinklehands

Julie was in the theater, sitting with her dad. The stage in front of her was dark and silent. Behind her, she could hear the rest of the audience chattering excitedly. What amazing magic would Peter Twinklehands perform tonight? Would he do his flying motorcycle trick?

Suddenly the stage began to fill up with green smoke. The audience became silent and everybody stared. With a flash of multicolored lights, Peter appeared right in the middle of the stage. The audience gasped.

"Good evening, my dear people," said Peter. His voice was soft but it sounded powerful. "I have many wonderful acts to perform for you tonight, so I should get started right away."

Peter suddenly leaned forward and pointed straight at Julie, his eyes wide and scary.

"You!" he said. "Do you want me to make your dad disappear?" He clapped his hands together and the whole theater echoed loudly.

Julie was scared. She turned to look at her dad, but he was gone! She panicked and wanted to cry. Where was her dad? She turned back to Peter to demand that he return her dad, but Peter was already getting ready for his next trick. "Bring out my motorcycle!" he called.

For the next couple of minutes, Julie watched the magic show, numb and scared. Suddenly a voice behind her said, "I bought you some popcorn." It was her dad!

From the stage, Peter looked down at her and winked.

Answer the questions.

1 How did the audience feel before the show started? Excited.

2 What did the audience do when Peter Twinklehands appeared? They gasped.

3 Did Peter Twinklehands really make Julie's dad disappear? How do you know?
No, he did not. Because Julie's dad came back with popcorn and then Peter winked at Julie.

Practice

Write a sentence from the story that shows mood.

1 scary
The stage in front of her was dark and silent.

3 sad
She panicked and wanted to cry.

Suggested answers
Students' answers can vary

2 exciting
Behind her, she could hear the rest of the audience chattering excitedly.

4 happy
From the stage, Peter looked down at her and winked.

Look for sentences that describe how people react or feel.

Look at the highlighted words in the story. Find out what they mean using the Mini-dictionary on pages 69–72.

Integration

G 6 **Read the sentences. Then identify the mood.**

1 The weather was bright and sunny, and the air smelled so fresh. happy
2 The girl walked slowly and heavily, looking down at her feet. sad
3 His eyes were shining, and his face was full of excitement. excited
4 She heard a noise behind her in the darkness. Her skin felt cold. scared

H Identify the mood in each photo. Then write a sentence that describes the mood.

1

Mood: sad

Sentence: Alone and confused, the girl sat on the floor.

2

Mood: scared

Sentence: The boy held the handles tight as the ride moved faster and faster.

Suggested answers
Students' answers can vary

I Write a sentence that describes your mood today. Then tell the class.

Mood: Excited

Sentence: Today my mother is coming home from a trip and I cannot wait to see her again.

Suggested answers
Students' answers can vary

Name: ______________________ Class: ______________ Date: ______________

Lost in Magic

When I was five years old, my mom and I were walking down the street one day when we saw a man in a black cape and top hat. There was a large crowd of people surrounding him. I wanted to see what he was doing so I told Mom. She said no—we were in a hurry and needed to go to the store to do the shopping.

I was really upset and started crying. Mom dragged me to the store, telling me to stop being a baby. At the store, Mom was busy shopping for groceries and not watching me. I decided to sneak away to see the man.

Outside, the man was doing card tricks. He asked people to pick cards and then to hide them. The cards would then appear in front of him again. It was magic! With each new trick something more amazing happened. When I realized that I had been gone a long time, I ran back to the store. But Mom was not there. I did not know what to do.

I ran outside and went up to the magician. I asked him if he could find my mom. Just then, I heard Mom calling my name. I turned around and saw her smiling at me. This time, I cried because I was so happy. The man really could do magic!

Write a sentence from the story that shows mood.

1 sad

____

____

2 scared

____

____

3 happy

____

____

4 excited

____

____

Read the passage.

The Magic Man

He can make the Statue of Liberty disappear. He can fly above the Grand Canyon. He can walk through the Great Wall of China. He is David Copperfield, one of the world's most talented and well-known magicians.

David showed his magical talents when he was young. At age 12, he started working as a magician and was the youngest person ever to join the Society of American Magicians. He taught a course in magic at New York University when he was just 16. By age 19, he was the star of his own magic show at a hotel in Hawaii.

In 2003, David was the tenth highest paid celebrity in the world, making more than $57 million. He likes to use his money to help others. He started Project Magic to help disabled people. He also built a museum in Las Vegas that shows magic equipment and books.

B **Underline the stated main idea in each paragraph. Then circle where in the paragraph it is.**

Paragraph 1: start / middle / (end)

Paragraph 2: (start) / middle / end

Paragraph 3: start / (middle) / end

Read the story.

Rob the Great Magician

Rob felt nervous. This was his first performance as a magician, even if it was just for his little sister's birthday party. He checked his magic hat to make sure the secret part at the bottom was still working. He practiced making a coin disappear and reappear using quick movements with his hands.

Everything seemed to be working. Still, Rob felt a little sick in his stomach. What if one of his tricks did not work? What if he looked like a fool in front of his sister's friends?

Rob began by pulling a toy rabbit out of the "empty" hat, and the children clapped and cheered. In another trick, he asked a little girl to help and made coins "appear" from behind her ear, in her pocket and even in her hair. The children made "ooh!" and "aah!" sounds as each new coin appeared. Rob felt the excitement!

After the show, Rob felt very good. Children were asking him to do more tricks, and his sister was proudly telling everyone about her brother—Rob the Great Magician.

D Check [✓] the word that best describes Rob's mood. Then underline words in the story that show the mood.

Paragraph 2:	sad		excited		worried	✓
Paragraph 3:	bored		excited	✓	scared	
Paragraph 4:	happy	✓	worried		sad	

Unit 3 Mission to Mars

Unit Overview

SUBJECT	Culture and People
READING SKILL	Cross-scanning for details
TEXT TYPE	Content-based passage

Reading Skill

Cross-scanning for details

Cross-scanning means looking from one side of a paragraph to another, instead of reading every word. It is an easier way of finding details. You cross-scan by looking at the words along the top of the paragraph, then diagonally down to the bottom. Next, look along the bottom of the paragraph, then diagonally back up to the top. You can also cross-scan a whole passage this way.

To provide students with cross-scanning practice, first prepare some questions that ask for specific information in a passage—you may wish to use one of the passages in the Student Book. In class, list the questions you want students to find the answers for. Have students identify the key word(s) in each question that they should look out for when they scan. Set the task up as a race and see how long it takes for students to find the answers.

Another activity is to have students cross-scan a passage and underline key words as they go along. When they have finished, have them write questions that would give those words as answers. Students can then ask classmates their questions to see if they get the correct answers.

Answers for Unit 3 Worksheet (p. 27)

1. Cross-scan for: manned — Answer: April 1961.
2. Cross-scan for: woman — Answer: Valentina Tereshkova.
3. Cross-scan for: moon mission — Answer: Apollo 11.
4. Cross-scan for: first — Answer: Yuri Gagarin.
5. Cross-scan for: step/leap — Answer: Neil Armstrong.
6. Cross-scan for: foot — Answer: July 20, 1969.
7. Cross-scan for: superpowers — Answer: The United States and the Soviet Union.

Mission to Mars

A **What do you know about the planet Mars? Discuss your answers.**

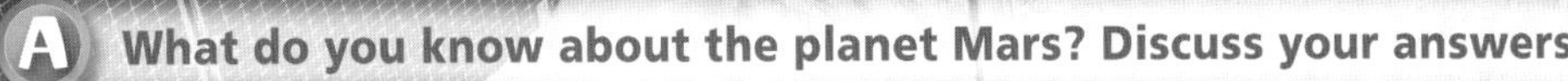

Reading Skill

Cross-scanning for details

Cross-scanning means looking from one side of a paragraph to another, instead of reading every word. It is an easier way of finding details.

B **Read the questions. Then cross-scan the paragraph by following the lines. You have 10 seconds to find and circle the answers.**

a Which agency sent the Viking robots to Mars?

b When was the Viking mission sent to Mars?

c What did the Viking robots measure?

d What did the Viking robot photograph?

1 One of the first successful missions 2
to Mars took place in 1976. In this
mission, two Viking robots were sent
by NASA, the U.S. space agency.
The Viking robots measured the
daily temperature and one of them
took a photograph of a hill that is
3 now known as the "face on Mars." 4

Read the passage.

Looking for Life on Mars

Scientists have long been interested in the planet Mars. It is one of the planets nearest to Earth and it is probably the most similar, too. Some scientists even think that humans can live on Mars in the future.

Over the past 40 years there have been many attempts to visit Mars to get information. Of the 37 attempts to reach Mars, 19 ended in disaster. Only six missions were able to send information back to Earth.

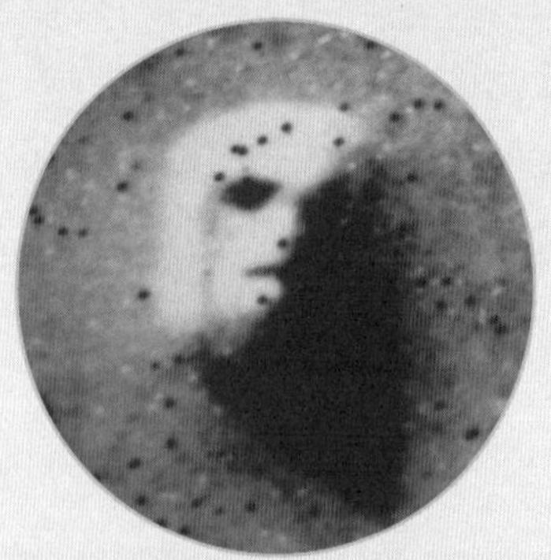

One of the first successful missions took place in 1976. In this mission, two Viking robots were sent to Mars by NASA, the U.S. space agency. The Viking robots measured the daily temperature and one of them took a photograph of a hill that is now known as the "face on Mars."

The most recent successful missions used rovers—special robots that can move around the surface of the planet. The rovers found proof that there was once a lot of water on Mars. This made scientists excited about the chance to show that life does (or did) exist on Mars.

The NASA rovers are still in good condition and continue to explore the surface of Mars.

D Answer the questions.

1 Why are scientists interested in Mars? Because Mars is one of the nearest planets and probably the most similar to Earth, they think that humans could live on Mars.

2 How many attempts have there been to reach Mars? 37.

3 What are rovers? Special robots that can move around.

Practice

E Cross-scan the paragraphs in the passage. You have 2 minutes to find and write the answers.

1 How many missions to Mars ended in disaster? 19.

2 What were the robots sent to Mars in 1976 called? Viking robots.

3 What do scientists think humans can do on Mars in the future? Live on Mars.

4 How many missions were able to send information back to Earth? Six.

5 How long have scientists been trying to visit Mars? 40 years.

6 What can rovers do? Move around the surface of the planet.

7 What did the rovers find proof of on Mars? Water.

8 What do the rovers continue to do now? Explore the surface of Mars.

9 What is the name of the U.S. space agency? NASA.

10 Why were scientists excited about finding water on Mars? It shows that life does (or did) exist on Mars.

TIP Underline the key words in each question and think about them as you cross-scan each paragraph.

F Look at the highlighted words in the passage. Find out what they mean using the Mini-dictionary on pages 69–72.

G 10 Should we continue to explore space? Cross-scan the dialogue and underline the reasons.

Yes, we should continue to explore space. There's still a lot that we don't know about other planets and one day we might find other forms of life. Also, maybe in the future we'll need another planet to live on, so we should continue looking.

No, exploring space costs a lot of money. Also, we still have many problems on our own planet and should work on those first. For example, we can try to find cures for diseases and we should give food to the poor. Those are more important than exploring space.

H Write what you and three classmates think about exploring space. Then tell the class.

Name	Yes	No	Reason
1 Me	✓		Earth is so polluted. We should look for another planet with cleaner air.
2 Bon-Hwa		✓	I think it is scary. Who knows what we will find on other planets? I like it here on Earth.
3 Jane		✓	It is a waste of money to explore space.
4 Tim	✓		It is cool. Just imagine being close to the stars.

Suggested answers
Students' answers can vary

Name: ______________________ Class: ______________ Date: ______________

The Race in Space

During the 1960s, the United States and the Soviet Union were the world's superpowers. They competed in everything—sports, business and, especially, space travel.

The Soviets were the first to enter space when, in April 1961, 27-year-old Yuri Gagarin completed the world's first manned space mission. He circled the Earth once in a 108-minute flight. In 1963, Valentina Tereshkova became the first woman in space, spending three days in her spaceship.

The United States wanted to be the first to explore the moon. On July 16, 1969, the moon mission Apollo 11 launched successfully. On July 20, astronauts Neil Armstrong and Buzz Aldrin began their trip down to the moon. When they landed, Armstrong got out, put one foot on the moon's surface and said, "That's one small step for man, one giant leap for mankind."

The space race between the United States and the Soviet Union—now known as Russia—continued for many more years. Nowadays, these two countries are working together. What will happen in the next 50 years? Hopefully there will be even greater space adventures.

Write the best key words or phrases to cross-scan for. Then cross-scan the passage and write the answers.

1 When was the first manned space mission?

Cross-scan for: ______________ Answer: ______________

2 Who was the first woman in space?

Cross-scan for: ______________ Answer: ______________

3 What was the name of the moon mission?

Cross-scan for: ______________ Answer: ______________

4 Who was the first man in space?

Cross-scan for: ______________ Answer: ______________

5 Who said "That's one small step for man, one giant leap for mankind."?

Cross-scan for: ______________ Answer: ______________

6 When did man first set foot on the moon?

Cross-scan for: ______________ Answer: ______________

7 Who were the world's superpowers in the 1960s?

Cross-scan for: ______________ Answer: ______________

____

Unit 4

The New Solar System

Unit Overview

SUBJECT	Science and Nature
READING SKILL	Finding information from tables
TEXT TYPE	Web article

Reading Skill

Finding information from tables

A table is the skeleton of information from a passage. It is usually used to present information that would not be clearly understood in paragraph form. Such information can include numerical data or a comparison between two or more things.

In general, people tend to look at an accompanying table before they read a passage. They do so to get a general sense of the information and to better understand the more difficult explanation in the passage.

As an activity, have students read a passage that talks about a few different things, such as the passage on magic in Unit 1. Get them to create a table that highlights key details from the passage.

Answers for Unit 4 Worksheet (p. 33)

1. A comparison between Earth and three other planets in the solar system.
2. Venus.
3. Jupiter.
4. Mars and Earth.
5. Mars.
6. Jupiter.
7. Mars and Venus.

The New Solar System

A What do you know about the planets that circle the Sun? Discuss your answers.

Reading Skill

Finding information from tables

Some information is best shown in tables than in paragraphs. Tables allow you to easily read and compare information.

B Complete the table using the information in the passage.

The planet Earth is 12,756 kilometers in diameter and 150 million kilometers from the Sun. It has an average temperature of 15 degrees Celsius. A year has 365 days and one day is 24 hours long.

Saturn, on the other hand, is 120,536 kilometers in diameter and 1,434 million kilometers from the Sun. It has an average surface temperature of –140 degrees Celsius. A year has 10,747 days and one day is about 10 hours and 42 minutes long.

Planet	Diameter (km)	Distance from the Sun (million km)	Average Temperature (°C)	Length of a Year (days)	Length of a Day (hrs. mins.)
Earth	12,756	150	15	365	24 hrs.
Saturn	120,536	1,434	–140	10,747	10 hrs. 42 mins.

11 **Read the article.**

www.astroinfo.com/news/story_G25L

Pluto is out!

For more than 76 years, we were told that there were nine planets circling the Sun, with Pluto being the last and most distant one. All that changed on August 24, 2006, when the world's astronomers decided that Pluto was no longer a planet. Now our solar system only has eight planets, not nine.

Pluto and its moon, Charon

Scientists have long been arguing about whether or not Pluto is really a planet. Questions about Pluto increased with the discovery of 2003 UB313, an icy object very far from the Sun. But scientists were also not sure if 2003 UB313, now formally known as Eris, should be called a planet.

Eventually, scientists decided that for an object to be classified as a planet, it must meet three criteria:

1 It must circle the Sun.
2 It must be large and round.
3 Its orbit must be free of other objects.

Both Pluto and Eris circle the Sun and are round. But their orbits are strange and are shared with other objects. For those reasons, they cannot be called planets. Instead, they are now called "dwarf planets."

Another object that was classified as a dwarf planet is Ceres, a huge round asteroid between Mars and Jupiter. Scientists expect to announce more dwarf planets in the future.

Dwarf Planet	Diameter (km)	Distance from the Sun (million km)	Average Temperature (°C)	Length of a Year (days)	Length of a Day (hours)
Pluto	2,390	5,870	–225	90,588	153
Eris	3,000	18,000	–300	203,550	8
Ceres	975	413	–106	1,680	9

24

D Answer the questions.

1 When did scientists decide that Pluto was no longer a planet? August 24, 2006.

2 What is Pluto now classified as? A dwarf planet.

3 What is 2003 UB313 formally known as? Eris.

Practice

E Look at the table and write the answers.

1 Which dwarf planet has the largest diameter? Eris.

2 Which dwarf planet has the smallest diameter? Ceres.

3 Which dwarf planet is the warmest? Ceres.

4 Which dwarf planet is the coldest? Eris.

5 Which dwarf planet has the shortest year? Ceres.

6 Which dwarf planet has the longest year? Eris.

7 Which dwarf planet has the shortest day? Eris.

8 Which dwarf planet has the longest day? Pluto.

9 How many days are there in a year on Pluto? 90,588.

10 Which dwarf planet is the closest to the Sun? Ceres.

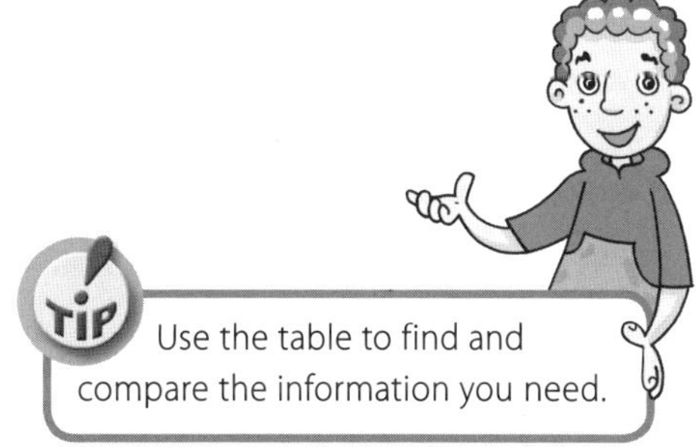

F Look at the highlighted words in the article. Find out what they mean using the Mini-dictionary on pages 69–72.

Integration

G 12 **Read the paragraph. Then write the missing information in the table.**

Mercury is the closest planet to the Sun, with a distance of 58 million kilometers. It has a surface temperature of 427 degrees Celsius during the day and –173 degrees Celsius at night. Venus is between Mercury and Earth. A year on Venus is 225 days long and each day lasts for 2,802 hours. Mars is 6,794 kilometers in diameter and is 228 million kilometers from the Sun. A day lasts for 24 hours and 42 minutes.

Answers for Activity G (Mercury–Mars)

Answers for Activity H (Jupiter–Neptune)

Planet	Diameter (km)	Distance from the Sun (million km)	Average Temperature (°C)	Length of a Year (days)	Length of a Day (hrs. mins.)
Mercury	4,879	58	427 (day) –173 (night)	88	4,222 hrs. 36 mins.
Venus	12,104	108	464	225	2,802 hrs.
Earth	12,756	150	15	365	24 hrs.
Mars	6,794	228	–65	687	24 hrs. 42 mins.
Jupiter	142,984	779	–110	4,331	9 hrs. 54 mins.
Saturn	120,536	1,434	–140	10,747	10 hrs. 42 mins.
Uranus	51,118	2,873	–195	30,589	17 hrs. 12 mins.
Neptune	49,528	4,495	–200	59,800	16 hrs. 6 mins.

H 13 **Listen and complete the table.**

H 13 *CD script on p. 96.*

I Write statements based on the information above. Then tell the class.

1 Jupiter is the biggest planet in the solar system.

2 A day on Mars is almost as long as a day on Earth.

3 Neptune is the farthest planet from the Sun.

Suggested answers
Students' answers can vary

Name: ____________________ Class: ____________ Date: ____________

Is life possible on other planets?

We know that Earth is suitable for life, but what exactly is it about Earth that allows people to live on it? Scientists believe that for life to exist on a planet, it must have the following:

- warmth
- elements like carbon, hydrogen and oxygen
- an atmosphere that protects life
- a water supply

Below is a comparison between Earth and three other planets in the solar system. We can see that although Jupiter has a thick atmosphere, its temperature is too cold and it does not have a water supply. After Earth, Mars seems to be the most suitable for life—it has water and it has an atmosphere (although it is thin). Venus is too hot for water or life.

Planet	Diameter (km)	Surface	Atmosphere	Temperature (°C)
Earth	12,756	solid rock, liquid water, carbon compounds	medium nitrogen and oxygen	15
Jupiter	142,984	liquid hydrogen	thick hydrogen and helium	–110
Mars	6,794	solid rock, ice	thin carbon dioxide	–65
Venus	12,104	solid rock	thick carbon dioxide	464

Look at the table and write the answers.

1 What does the table show? ____________________

____

2 Which is the hottest planet? ____________________

3 Which is the largest planet? ____________________

4 Which two planets have water? ____________________

5 Which planet is the smallest? ____________________

6 Which planet has no land surface? ____________________

7 Which two planets have an atmosphere that is mostly made up of the same gas?

____

Photocopiable

Read the passage.

Would life on Mars be better?

Problems on our own planet Earth make a lot of people think that we may need to find a new planet to live on. Of the planets in the solar system, Mars is the most popular choice. It is very similar to Earth, which is why life on Mars might be easier than on other planets.

The Martian and Earth days are almost the same—a day on Mars is about 24 hours. Mars and Earth have about the same land surface area. Both have an atmosphere and water. Mars also has seasons, just like Earth. These similarities mean that life on Mars for humans could be possible—it could be close to the life humans have on Earth.

However, the differences between Mars and Earth make living on Mars challenging. There are 687 days in each Martian year and each season would be nearly twice as long as an Earth season. Even though Mars has an atmosphere, it is very thin and is mainly carbon dioxide—there is not enough oxygen for humans to breathe! There is little water on Mars and it could be very hard to find. Also, it is very cold on Mars and gravity is weaker.

	Earth	Mars
Diameter	12,756 km	6,794 km
Land Surface Area	149 million km^2	145 million km^2
Distance from the Sun	150 million km	228 million km
Average Temperature	15°C	–65°C
Length of a Year	365 days	687 days
Length of a Day	24 hrs.	24 hrs. 42 mins.

Review 2

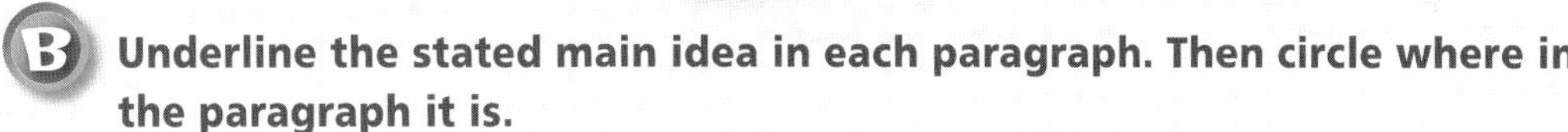

B **Underline the stated main idea in each paragraph. Then circle where in the paragraph it is.**

Paragraph 1: start / middle / end

Paragraph 2: start / middle / end

Paragraph 3: start / middle / end

C **Cross-scan the paragraphs in the passage and write the answers.**

1 How are Martian and Earth seasons different?
A Martian season would be nearly twice as long as an Earth season.

2 Is the Martian atmosphere thick or thin?
Thin.

3 What does Earth have that Mars does not have?
A lot of water and oxygen.

4 What do the differences between Mars and Earth mean?
Living on Mars would be challenging.

D **Look at the table and write the answers.**

1 Which planet has a larger diameter? Earth.

2 Which planet is farther from the Sun? Mars.

3 Which planet is colder? Mars.

4 Is the length of a year on Mars and Earth similar or different? Different.

5 Is the length of a day on Mars and Earth similar or different? Similar.

28

Unit 5

Connecting Continents

Unit Overview

SUBJECT	Social Studies
READING SKILL	Understanding settings
TEXT TYPE	Content-based passage

Reading Skill

Understanding settings

Setting is the time, place and situation in a passage. Knowing the setting helps you identify things that happened in the past, are real in the present or possible in the future.

Having students look at the verbs in a passage will help them get a clear idea of when events happened. Have them circle the verbs and decide whether they are past, present or future. This will indicate the setting. Remind students that the setting can change from sentence to sentence and sometimes even within a sentence.

Students must also look for phrases with dates and times. But warn them that such phrases could be confusing. For example, *in winter* indicates present time even though it may currently be spring.

Have students look for details that tell where a story takes place to identify the setting—this will help put an image in their heads. They must pay attention to descriptive words.

Answers for Unit 5 Worksheet (p. 41)

A

1. Cross-scan for: complete — Answer: Seven years.
2. Cross-scan for: passenger service — Answer: London, Paris and Brussels.
3. Cross-scan for: nickname — Answer: The Chunnel.

B

1. Past
2. Present
3. Future
4. Past
5. Present
6. Past

Connecting Continents

A What is exciting about traveling around the world? Discuss your answers.

Reading Skill

Understanding settings

Setting is the time, place and situation in a passage. Knowing the setting helps you identify things that happened in the past, are real in the present or possible in the future.

B Circle the correct setting.

1

The Bering Strait is the sea that separates Alaska from Siberia. The strait is narrow—it is only about 85 km wide. Winters in the strait are long and dark, with the temperature going down as low as –50 degrees Celsius.

past / present / future

2

A bridge connecting Asia and the Americas would be very special. People would be able to travel easily from one side of the world to the other. Trade would increase, and people could learn about other cultures more easily. For these reasons, this bridge would be called the Intercontinental Peace Bridge.

past / present / future

Reading

15 **Read the passage.**

Bridge to Tomorrow

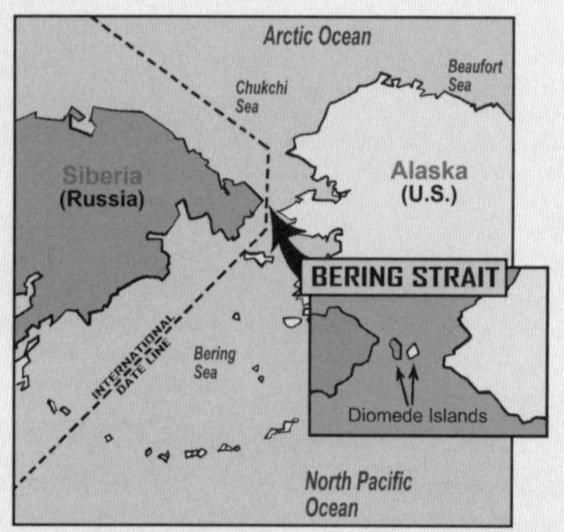

The Bering Strait is the sea that separates Alaska from Siberia. The strait is narrow—it is only about 85 km wide. Winters in the strait are long and dark, with the temperature going down as low as –50 degrees Celsius.

In the middle of the strait are two islands known as the Diomede Islands. The International Date Line runs between the Diomede Islands. This means that from "today" on Little Diomede (on the Alaskan side) you can look across at "tomorrow" on Big Diomede (on the Siberian side). This is also the line that separates the Americas from Asia. Thousands of years ago, these two continents were connected. Lower sea levels during the Ice Age showed a huge land that joined them. People then crossed over from Asia to live all over the Americas.

People are now saying that it is time to connect the continents again. To do this, a huge bridge would need to be built. Of course, it would not be easy. The bridge would take a long time to build and cost billions of dollars. It would need to be strong to withstand icebergs and winter winds. Also, it would probably only be usable during the summer months.

But the bridge would be very special. People would be able to travel easily from one side of the world to the other. Trade would increase, and people could learn about other cultures more easily. For these reasons, this bridge would be called the Intercontinental Peace Bridge.

D Answer the questions.

1 What does the Bering Strait separate? Alaska and Siberia; Asia and the Americas.

2 How wide is the Bering Strait? 85 km.

3 Why can you see tomorrow from Little Diomede? The International Date Line runs between Little Diomede and Big Diomede.

E Check [✓] the statements that show *Past*, *Present* or *Future*.

		Past	Present	Future
1	A bridge connecting Alaska and Siberia would take a long time to build.			✓
2	The Bering Strait is the sea that separates Alaska and Siberia.		✓	
3	Thousands of years ago, Asia and the Americas were connected.	✓		
4	People would be able to travel easily from one side of the world to the other.			✓
5	People crossed over from Asia to live all over the Americas.	✓		
6	People could learn about other cultures more easily.			✓
7	From "today" on Little Diomede, you can look across at "tomorrow" on Big Diomede.		✓	
8	Lower sea levels during the Ice Age showed a huge land connecting Asia and Americas.	✓		

Look for words that show present (is, can, has), past (were) and future (would) settings.

F Look at the highlighted words in the passage. Find out what they mean using the Mini-dictionary on pages 69–72.

Integration

16 **Read the paragraph. Write details that show *Present* and *Future*.**

I think building the Intercontinental Peace Bridge is impossible. Just think of the icebergs in the Bering Strait. The icebergs would just destroy the bridge pillars. Also, there are no roads or railways in Alaska or Siberia that go all the way to the coasts—thousands of kilometers of new roads and railway tracks would have to be built.

	Present		Future
1	Icebergs are in the strait.	1	The icebergs would destory the bridge pillars.
2	There are no roads or railways in Alaska or Siberia that go to the coasts.	2	New roads and railway tracks would have to be built.

17 **Listen and complete the paragraph.**

I think we can build the (1) Intercontinental Peace Bridge. If the bridge pillars are very (2) big and shaped like ice-breaking (3) ships, they could (4) withstand icebergs. Russia has already made railways that are almost (5) 10,000 km long. So it is possible to make railways that are (6) long enough to reach the coasts.

Work with a classmate. On a separate piece of paper, design a bridge that connects Asia and the Americas. Then present it to the class.

Name: ______________________ Class: ______________ Date: ______________

Channel Tunnel

The Channel Tunnel is a tunnel under the English Channel that extends from England to France. With a length of 50 kilometers, it is the second longest tunnel in the world and the longest undersea tunnel. It is known by its nickname, the Chunnel.

The tunnel project was long and expensive. Digging started in 1987. There were 15,000 workers, with operations starting on both the English and French ends. The tunnel took seven years to complete. It was officially opened by Queen Elizabeth II and the French President François Mitterrand in a ceremony held on May 6, 1994.

The Channel Tunnel offers three kinds of services: a shuttle service for vehicles, a passenger service linking London with Paris and Brussels, and a freight train service. A journey through the tunnel takes about 20 minutes; from start to end, a shuttle train journey totals about 35 minutes. A second tunnel could be built if there is ever a need for one.

A Write the best key words or phrases to cross-scan for. Then cross-scan the passage and write the answers.

1 How long did it take to complete the Channel Tunnel?

Cross-scan for: ______________ Answer: ______________

2 Which cities does the passenger service connect?

Cross-scan for: ______________ Answer: ______________

3 What is the Channel Tunnel's nickname?

Cross-scan for: ______________ Answer: ______________

B Check [✓] the statements that show *Past*, *Present* or *Future*.

		Past	Present	Future
1	The tunnel took seven years to complete.			
2	The Channel Tunnel is a tunnel under the English Channel that extends from England to France.			
3	A second tunnel could be built if there is ever a need for one.			
4	The tunnel project was long and expensive.			
5	It is known by its nickname, the Chunnel.			
6	It was officially opened by Queen Elizabeth II and the French President François Mitterrand.			

Unit 6 Sightseeing

Unit Overview

SUBJECT	Social Studies
READING SKILL	Understanding brochures
TEXT TYPE	Brochure

Reading Skill

Understanding brochures

A brochure is a thin book that gives information about a product or service. It is a good way of finding out information without doing a lot of research. Brochures are usually an advertisement of some kind. People sometimes hand them out on the street. Well-planned brochures can make you want to buy something.

Download brochures for products or services from the websites of department stores, travel agencies, etc., and print them out. Have students read through the brochures and discuss them. Then have them write down important information such as the product or service offered, prices, dates and contact details.

Afterward, have students write and design their own brochures. Make sure they include key information such as prices, schedules or things that come with the package.

Answers for Unit 6 Worksheet (p. 47)

1. A sightseeing and cruise tour of Egypt.
2. $1,800 per person.
3. Ten days.
4. Ten people.
5. No.
6. Airport taxes, visa fees, optional tours and tips.

Unit 6 Sightseeing

A What are your favorite tourist spots? Discuss your answers.

Reading Skill

Understanding brochures

A brochure is a thin book that gives information about a product or a service. Well-planned brochures can make you want to buy something.

B Label the parts of the brochure. Write the letter.

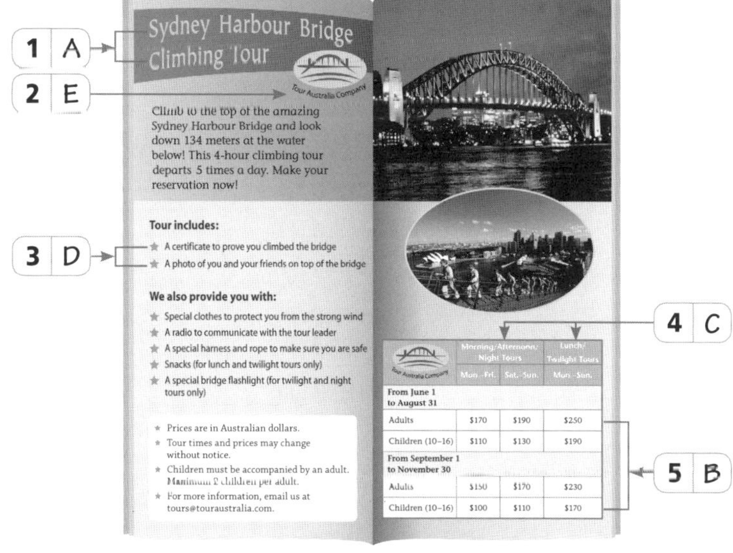

Sydney Harbour Bridge Climbing Tour

Tour Australia Company

Climb to the top of the amazing Sydney Harbour Bridge and look down 134 meters at the water below! This 4-hour climbing tour departs 5 times a day. Make your reservation now!

Tour includes:

- A certificate to prove you climbed the bridge
- A photo of you and your friends on top of the bridge

We also provide you with:

- Special clothes to protect you from the strong wind
- A radio to communicate with the tour leader
- A special harness and rope to make sure you are safe
- Snacks (for lunch and twilight tours only)
- A special bridge flashlight (for twilight and night tours only)

- Prices are in Australian dollars.
- Tour times and prices may change without notice.
- Children must be accompanied by an adult. Maximum 2 children per adult.
- For more information, email us at tours@touraustralia.com.

Tour Australia Company	Morning/Afternoon/Night Tours		Lunch/Twilight Tours
	Mon.–Fri.	Sat.–Sun.	Mon.–Sun.
From June 1 to August 31			
Adults	$170	$190	$250
Children (10–16)	$110	$130	$190
From September 1 to November 30			
Adults	$150	$170	$230
Children (10–16)	$100	$110	$170

A name of tour
B cost of tour
C tours offered
D what you get after the tour
E name of the tour company

18 **Read the brochure.**

Sydney Harbour Bridge Climbing Tour

Tour Australia Company

Climb to the top of the amazing Sydney Harbour Bridge and look down 134 meters at the water below! This 4-hour climbing tour departs 5 times a day. Make your reservation now!

Tour includes:

- A certificate to prove you climbed the bridge
- A photo of you and your friends on top of the bridge

We also provide you with:

- Special clothes to protect you from the strong wind
- A radio to communicate with the tour leader
- A special harness and rope to make sure you are safe
- Snacks (for lunch and twilight tours only)
- A special bridge flashlight (for twilight and night tours only)

- Prices are in Australian dollars.
- Tour times and prices may change without notice.
- Children must be accompanied by an adult. Maximum 2 children per adult.
- For more information, email us at tours@touraustralia.com.

Tour Australia Company	Morning/Afternoon/ Night Tours		Lunch/ Twilight Tours
	Mon.–Fri.	Sat.–Sun.	Mon.–Sun.
From June 1 to August 31			
Adults	$170	$190	$250
Children (10–16)	$110	$130	$190
From September 1 to November 30			
Adults	$150	$170	$230
Children (10–16)	$100	$110	$170

Practice

D **Write the answers.**

1 What kind of tour does the brochure advertise? Climbing tour.

2 How much does it cost for a 12-year-old child to take a twilight tour in August?
$190.

3 How many tours are offered every day? 5.

4 How long does the tour last? 4 hours.

5 How high above the water does the tour take people? 134 meters.

6 What does the tour include? A certificate and photo.

7 What are provided to ensure safety on the tours?
Special clothes, radio, harness, rope and flashlight.

8 What is not provided for the night tour? Snacks.

9 How much would it cost for one adult and two children to take an afternoon tour on a Sunday in November? $390.

10 Can children go on the tour by themselves? No.

11 Why does a person get a certificate after the tour? To prove he/she climbed the bridge.

12 In which months are the prices lower? September, October and November.

E **Look at the highlighted words in the brochure. Find out what they mean using the Mini-dictionary on pages 69–72.**

Integration

Read the notes about the Sydney Harbour Bridge climbing tour. Then write out some of the notes as questions.

- children aged 9?
- Tour guides / languages?
- certificates / look like?

- older sister / 17?
- special shoes?
- if it rains?

- $ / 1 Sep to 30 Nov. / why?
- digital camera / allowed?
- camcorder / safe?

1 Can children aged 9 take the tour?

2 What do the certificates look like?

3 How much does it cost for my 17-year-old sister to take the tour?

4 Do I need to wear special shoes for the tour?

5 Am I allowed to take my digital camera with me?

6 Will it be safe to take a camcorder?

Suggested answers
Students' answers can vary

G **On a separate piece of paper, write a letter to the tour company asking the questions above. Then read your letter to the class.**

Name: ________________ Class: ________________ Date: ________________

SUNNY WORLD TOURS

10-day Tour of Egypt
Cairo, Aswan and Luxor

Tour includes:

- Round trip flight to Cairo and domestic destinations
- 4-night Nile cruise on an Egyptian riverboat
- 1 night in Luxor
- 3 nights in Cairo
- Accommodation in 4-star hotels
- All meals included
- Sightseeing
- Services of an English-speaking Egyptologist tour guide
- Entrance fees

Attractions:

King Tut Collection, Egyptian Museum, Valley of the Kings & Queens, King's Chamber, Great Pyramid and the Sphinx, Temples of Karnak

Jun. 1–Aug. 30 / Dec. 1–Feb. 28
$1,800 per person

Mar. 1–May 31 / Sept. 1–Nov. 30
$1,500 per person

- Maximum number of people per tour is 10.
- Children must be accompanied by an adult.
- Airport taxes, visa fees, optional tours & tips are not included.
- Most travelers will need a visa for this trip.
- For more information, email us at egypttours@sunnyworldtours.com

Write the answers.

1 What kind of tour does the brochure advertise? ________________

2 How much does it cost to take a tour in January? ________________

3 How long is the tour? ________________

4 How many people are allowed per tour? ________________

5 Can children travel by themselves? ________________

6 What is not included? ________________

Review 3

A 19 **Read the brochure.**

Take the Millau Viaduct bicycle tour!

Feel what it's like to fly like a bird above the morning clouds ...

We provide the bicycle, protective gear and a guide who will tell you all about the bridge.

Saturdays, Sundays and public holidays only.

Prices:

Adults: 15 Euros

Children (9–15): 12 Euros

Note: Children must be accompanied by an adult.

The History of the Millau Viaduct

In 1989, the French government was looking for a way to solve the traffic problem in the Tarn Valley. Officials wanted to build a new bridge to stop the cars from getting stuck in the valley. But they were worried about building something that might destroy the scenery or upset the people who lived in the valley.

In December 2004, the Millau Viaduct opened. The bridge is so beautiful that it almost looks like a natural part of the valley. With some parts of the bridge taller than the Eiffel Tower, tourists (numbering 10,000–25,000 every day) can drive on the bridge and feel like they are flying over the valley. Below the bridge, the valley's people are enjoying life with fewer cars and less pollution.

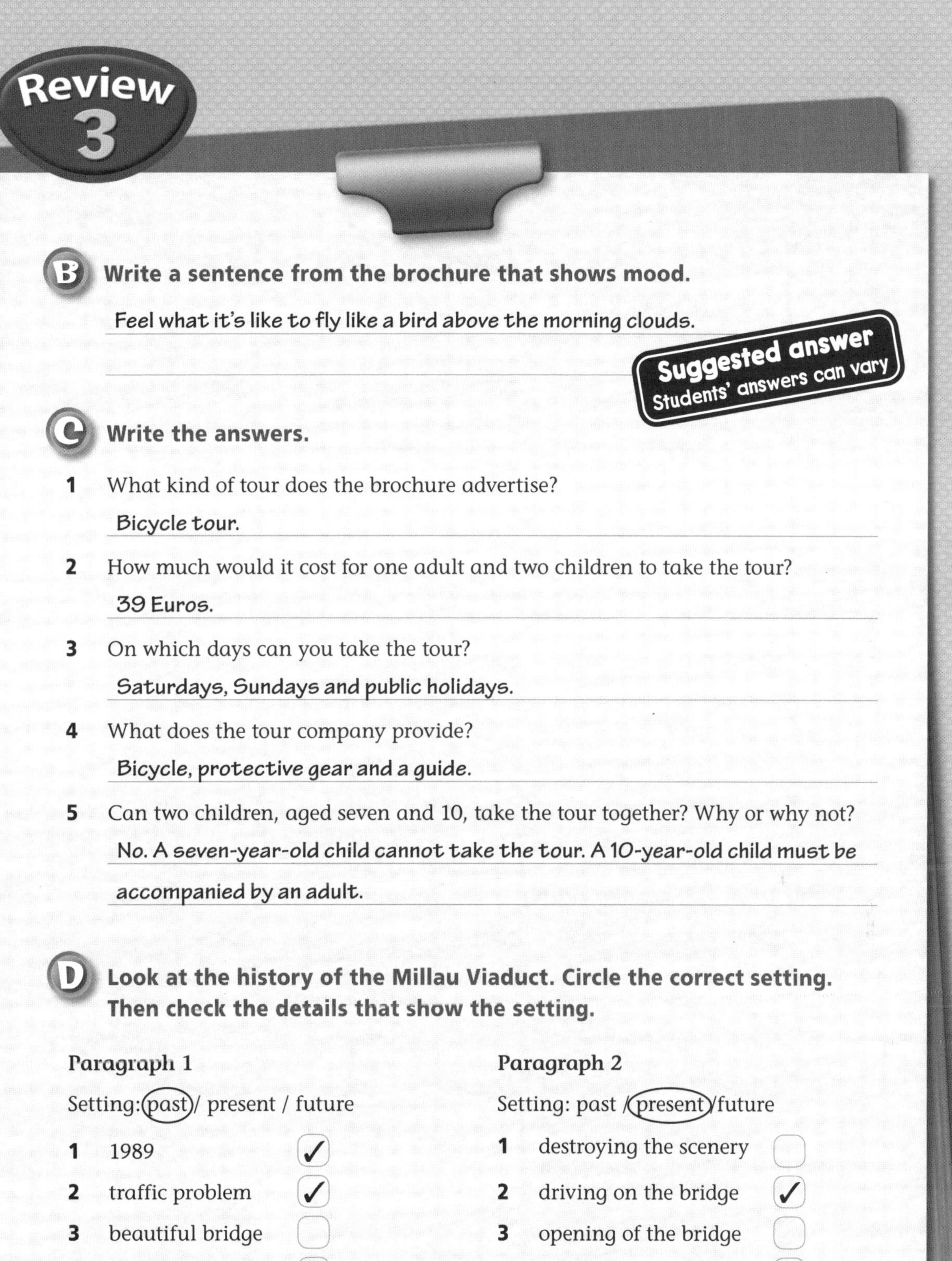

Review 3

B **Write a sentence from the brochure that shows mood.**

Feel what it's like to fly like a bird above the morning clouds.

Suggested answer
Students' answers can vary

C **Write the answers.**

1 What kind of tour does the brochure advertise?
Bicycle tour.

2 How much would it cost for one adult and two children to take the tour?
39 Euros.

3 On which days can you take the tour?
Saturdays, Sundays and public holidays.

4 What does the tour company provide?
Bicycle, protective gear and a guide.

5 Can two children, aged seven and 10, take the tour together? Why or why not?
No. A seven-year-old child cannot take the tour. A 10-year-old child must be accompanied by an adult.

D **Look at the history of the Millau Viaduct. Circle the correct setting. Then check the details that show the setting.**

Paragraph 1

Setting: (past) / present / future

1 1989 ✓
2 traffic problem ✓
3 beautiful bridge ☐
4 2004 ☐

Paragraph 2

Setting: past / (present) / future

1 destroying the scenery ☐
2 driving on the bridge ✓
3 opening of the bridge ☐
4 less pollution ✓

Unit 7 The Olympics

Unit Overview

SUBJECT	History/Sports and Leisure
READING SKILL	Understanding summaries
TEXT TYPE	Content-based passage

Reading Skill

Understanding summaries

A summary states the main ideas in a passage in just a few sentences. Good summaries use simple words and short sentences. The ideas do not really need to be in the same order as in the text, but it is best to mention the strongest ideas first.

To help students understand summaries, have them read just one paragraph of a passage and list the important details in the paragraph. Have them write down the most important thing they learned from the paragraph. This should summarize the paragraph. Continue to do this with the other paragraphs. At the end, have students build a summary of the whole passage from the individual paragraph summaries.

For reversed practice, have students write two or three short sentences that relate to each other. Using these as the summary, have them write a full paragraph.

Answers for Unit 7 Worksheet (p. 55)

Paragraph 2

1. The Paralympic Games started as an event for injured soldiers.

3. There are different types of events in the games.

Paragraph 3

2. The games happen in the same place and year as the Olympics.

4. Both the Olympics and the Paralympics have the same organizers.

The Olympics

Unit 7

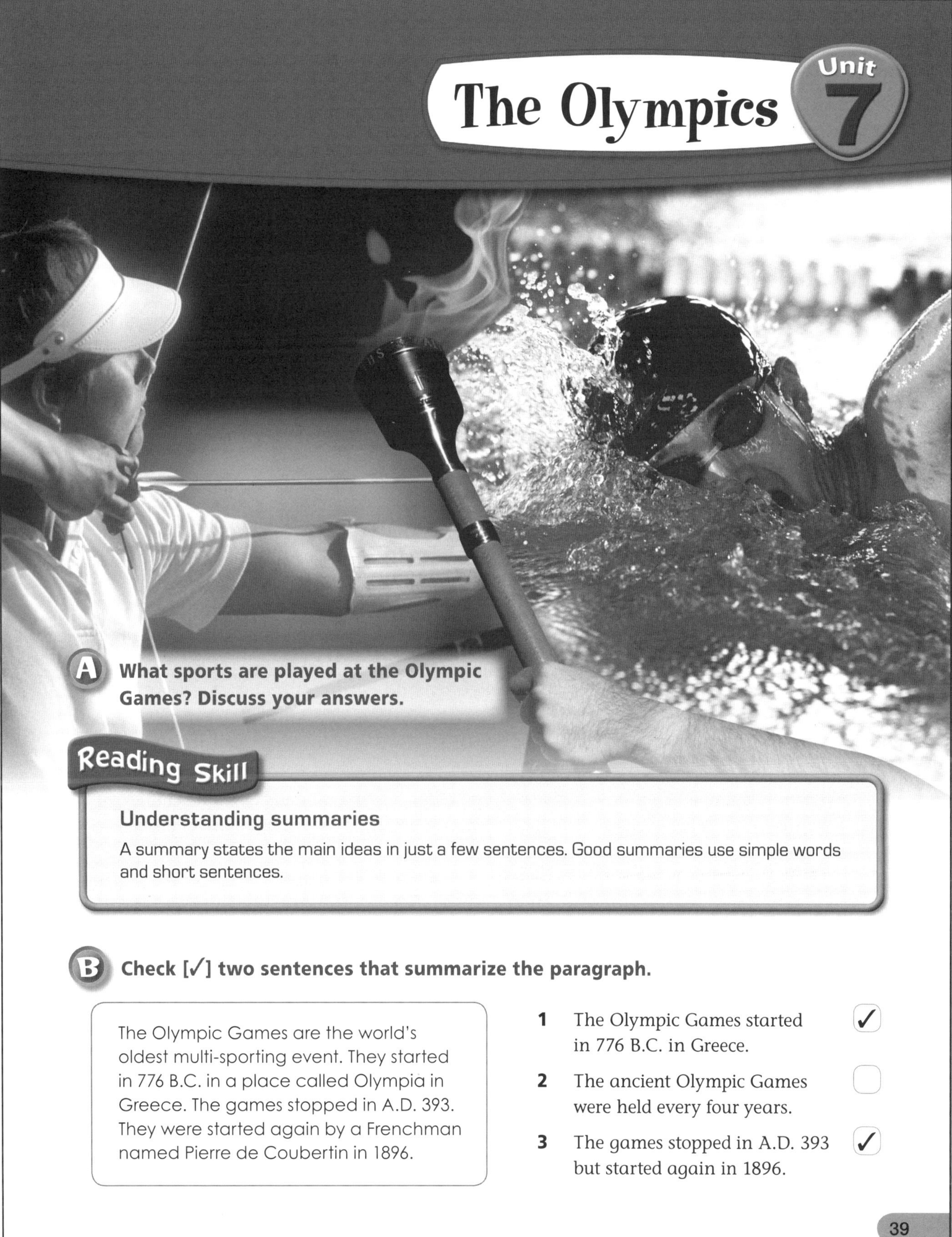

A **What sports are played at the Olympic Games? Discuss your answers.**

Reading Skill

Understanding summaries

A summary states the main ideas in just a few sentences. Good summaries use simple words and short sentences.

B **Check [✓] two sentences that summarize the paragraph.**

The Olympic Games are the world's oldest multi-sporting event. They started in 776 B.C. in a place called Olympia in Greece. The games stopped in A.D. 393. They were started again by a Frenchman named Pierre de Coubertin in 1896.

1. The Olympic Games started in 776 B.C. in Greece. [✓]
2. The ancient Olympic Games were held every four years. [ ]
3. The games stopped in A.D. 393 but started again in 1896. [✓]

Read the passage.

The History of the Olympic Games

The Olympic Games are the world's oldest multisporting event. They started in 776 B.C. in a place called Olympia in Greece. The games stopped in A.D. 393, but started again in 1896.

The Ancient Olympics

According to stories, King Ifitos of Elis in Greece started the games as a way to stop the fighting among Greek kingdoms. Instead of fighting, the warriors competed in sporting events. There were about 20 events and only Greek men could join. It cost a lot of money to train for and travel to the games. Winners received a crown of olive leaves and often had poems written or statues made in their honor.

The Modern Olympics

A Frenchman named Pierre de Coubertin organized the first modern Olympic Games. He wanted to promote sports and thought it would be better for young men to compete than fight. The first games were held in Athens in 1896 and had 245 participants from 15 nations. At the time it was the biggest international sporting event. The recent games in Athens involved 11,100 participants from 202 countries.

The modern Olympic Games are held every four years. These are divided into the Summer and Winter Games, which are held two years apart. Winners get a gold, silver or bronze medal.

40

D Answer the questions.

1. When did the ancient Olympic Games stop? A.D. 393.
2. Who could compete in the ancient Olympic Games? Greek men.
3. How many nations competed at the recent Olympic Games in Athens? 202.

Practice

E Check [✓] two sentences that summarize each paragraph.

Paragraph 2

1. Warriors competed in sporting events. [ ]
2. The ancient Olympic Games were meant to stop the fighting among Greek kingdoms. [✓]
3. Winners were made famous through poems or statues. [✓]
4. King Ifitos of Elis in Greece started the games. [ ]

Paragraph 3

1. The modern Olympic Games were started in 1896 by Pierre de Coubertin. [✓]
2. The first games were held in Athens. [ ]
3. The modern Olympic Games have grown hugely in the number of participants. [✓]
4. Pierre de Coubertin wanted to promote sports. [ ]

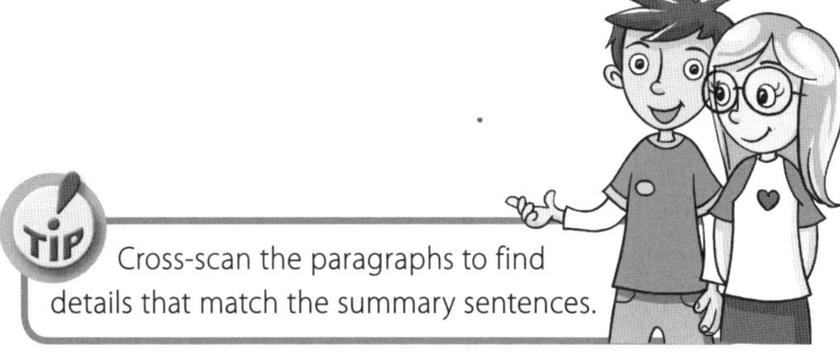

F Look at the highlighted words in the passage. Find out what these words mean using the Mini-dictionary on pages 69–72.

Integration

21 Read the dialogue about the Olympic Games. Then write a summary of each paragraph.

I think the Olympic Games are a good thing. They get people from different nations to compete in a way that's fun and not dangerous. This encourages people to share ideas. This way, they can learn to understand one another better.

The Olympic Games are good because they bring together people from many nations. The games help people understand one another.

Suggested answer
Students' answers can vary

I don't think the Olympic Games are important. I don't see how we can better understand people of other cultures when we're competing with them—we would be too busy thinking about winning. I think it's easier to learn about other cultures through real friendships than through "friendly" competitions. Through friendships, we learn to respect our differences.

The Olympic Games are not important. It's easier to learn about other cultures through friendships than competitions.

Suggested answer
Students' answers can vary

H What do you think is good about the Olympic Games? Tell the class.

Name: ______________________ Class: ______________ Date: ______________

The Paralympics

The Paralympic Games are a multisporting event for athletes with physical disabilities. They are held every four years, after the Olympics. Athletes belong to these six different groups:

- people who have had an arm or leg removed
- people born with cerebral palsy and, therefore, have trouble moving their arms, legs or bodies
- people who are blind
- people with spinal cord injuries and, therefore, cannot move and feel most parts of their bodies
- people with limited thinking skills
- people with disabilities that do not fit into the above five groups

The games started in 1952 when Sir Ludwig Guttmann organized an event for soldiers injured during World War II. In 1960 the first Olympic-style games for disabled athletes were held in Rome. Today, the Paralympic Games are divided into summer and winter games. Summer games include wheelchair sports, track and field, archery and swimming. Winter games include skiing, ice sled hockey and wheelchair curling. The top three participants receive gold, silver and bronze medals respectively.

The games take place three weeks after the closing of the Olympics. They are held in the same host city and use the same facilities. Cities competing to host the Olympic Games must include the Paralympic Games in their bid. Both games are usually organized by a single committee.

Check [✓] two sentences that summarize each paragraph.

Paragraph 2

1 The Paralympic Games started as an event for injured soldiers. ☐

2 The first Olympic-style games for disabled athletes were in 1960. ☐

3 There are different types of events in the games. ☐

4 Winners receive gold, silver or bronze medals. ☐

Paragraph 3

1 The Paralympics begin three weeks after the Olympics close. ☐

2 The games happen in the same place and year as the Olympics. ☐

3 Host cities include the Paralympics in their bids. ☐

4 Both the Olympics and the Paralympics have the same organizers. ☐

Unit 8 Meet an Olympian!

Unit Overview

SUBJECT	Culture and People
READING SKILL	Identifying character
TEXT TYPE	Magazine article

Reading Skill

Identifying character

Character is what a person is like. Is the person brave, weak, smart or silly? Knowing people's character helps you better understand the passage and predict what might happen next.

Clues about character are often found in the paragraphs. You need to think about what the people in the passage say and their actions to find out what they are like. Have students discuss what the people in the passage will do next and why they think they will do that. Also have students notice how people act toward each other in the passage.

Have students write down five adjectives of their choice. Next, have them work in groups and brainstorm ideas that can support those adjectives. For example, *brave — not scared of anything, a soldier, likes dangerous things, climbed Mount Everest.* Have students compare their ideas with other groups.

Answers for Unit 8 Worksheet (p. 61)

A

	Scott's character	Supporting detail
1	passionate about the sport	loves curling and considers it a lifetime sport
2	likes learning	watches younger athletes at play and learns from them
3	experienced	been curling since 1961

B

1. Past
2. Present
3. Future

Meet an Olympian!

Unit 8

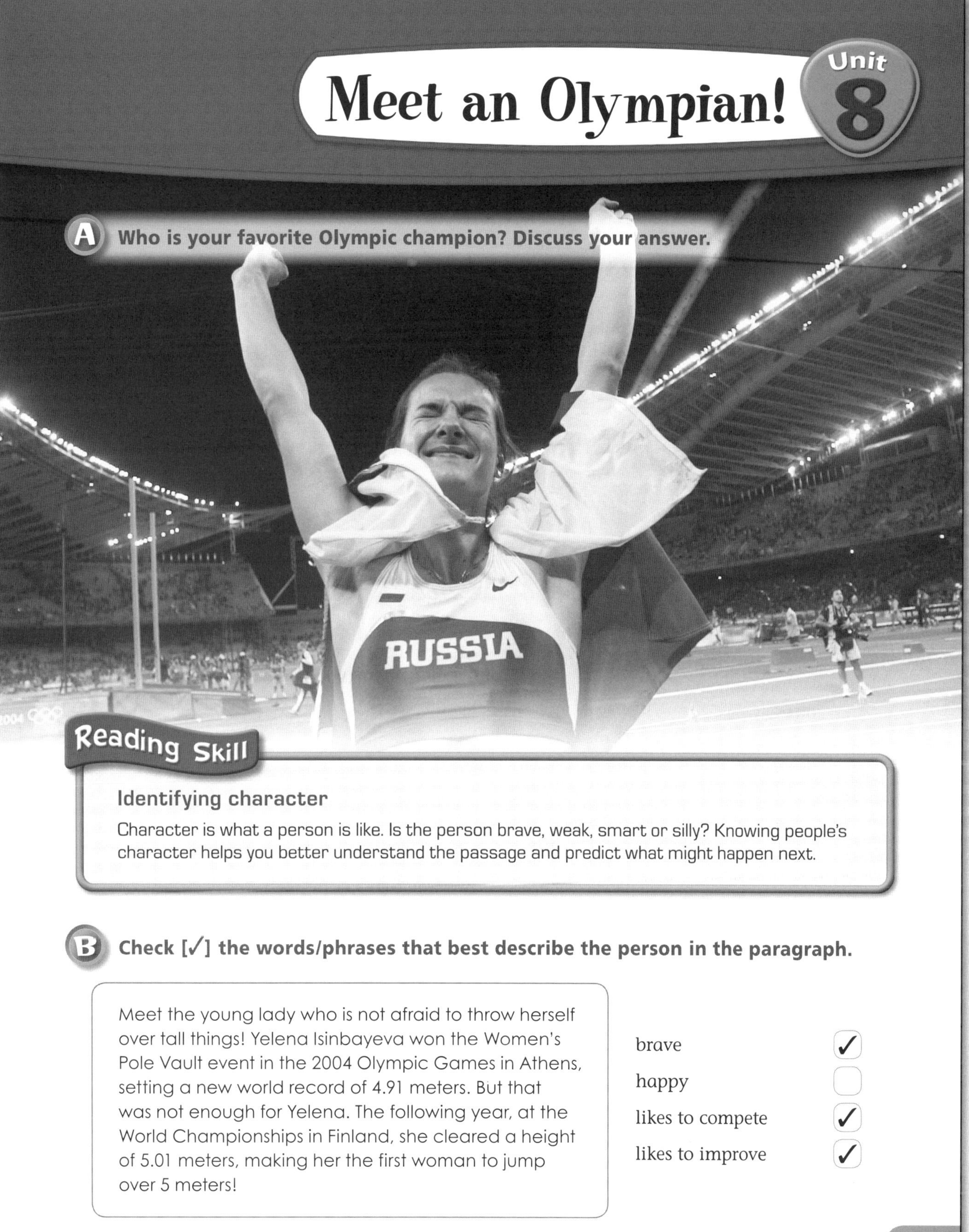

A Who is your favorite Olympic champion? Discuss your answer.

Reading Skill

Identifying character

Character is what a person is like. Is the person brave, weak, smart or silly? Knowing people's character helps you better understand the passage and predict what might happen next.

B Check [✓] the words/phrases that best describe the person in the paragraph.

Meet the young lady who is not afraid to throw herself over tall things! Yelena Isinbayeva won the Women's Pole Vault event in the 2004 Olympic Games in Athens, setting a new world record of 4.91 meters. But that was not enough for Yelena. The following year, at the World Championships in Finland, she cleared a height of 5.01 meters, making her the first woman to jump over 5 meters!

- brave ✓
- happy ☐
- likes to compete ✓
- likes to improve ✓

22 **Read the article.**

▶profile

Yelena Isinbayeva

Queen of the Leap

Meet the young lady who is not afraid to throw herself over tall things! Yelena Isinbayeva won the Women's Pole Vault event in the 2004 Olympic Games in Athens, setting a new world record of 4.91 meters. But that was not enough for Yelena. The following year, at the World Championships in Finland, she cleared a height of 5.01 meters, making her the first woman to jump over 5 meters!

Yelena was born in Russia on June 3, 1982. She started out doing gymnastics when she was five years old. However, by the time she was 15 she was too tall and was encouraged to try pole vaulting instead. Her gymnastics training helped her in this new event. Soon, she was breaking world records.

Yelena is very close to her family. One time, her parents banned her from driving because they were worried that she might get hurt. She rode the streetcar instead! She still lives with her parents and younger sister in her hometown of Volgograd. When she is not training, she likes to help her mother in the kitchen.

Yelena has a Bachelor's degree. Believe it or not, she is also a member of the Russian army and holds the rank of Senior Lieutenant. She dreams of opening a restaurant someday.

D Answer the questions.

1 How old is Yelena now? [Answer will depend on the year the book is used.]

2 What did Yelena achieve at the 2004 Olympic Games? She won the Women's Pole Vault event and set a new world record.

3 Why did Yelena's parents ban her from driving? Because they were worried that she might get hurt.

E Write details from the article that support the descriptions.

Yelena's character	Supporting details
1 willing to try new things	tried pole vaulting
2 thinks about her future	dreams of opening a restaurant someday
3 loves her family	still lives with her parents and younger sister
4 likes cooking	likes to help her mother in the kitchen
5 values education	has a Bachelor's degree
6 likes discipline	a member of the Russian army

F Look at the highlighted words in the article. Find out what they mean using the Mini-dictionary on pages 69–72.

G 23 **Read about Shizuka Arakawa. Then check [✓] the questions that show interesting things about her character.**

Name: Shizuka Arakawa
Date of birth: December 29, 1981
Place of birth: Sendai, Japan
Height: 166 cm
Famous for:
- Winning Japan's first ever Olympic gold medal in figure-skating, at the 2006 Winter Olympic Games in Turin, Italy
- Being the first female skater born in Asia to win an Olympic gold medal in figure skating

1 When did you decide to become a figure skater? ✓
2 How long did it take you to become good at figure skating? ✓
3 What is your favorite city? ☐
4 How many hours a day do you train? ✓
5 Who is your best friend? ☐
6 What do you like to do in your free time? ✓

H **Think of an athlete who you would like to interview. Write questions that will show his/her character. Then tell the class.**

1 How did you get started in boxing?
2 What is it about boxing that you like?
3 How does your family feel about your love for boxing?
4 How did boxing change your life?
5 Which boxers do you look up to and why?
6 If you weren't a boxer, what would you be?

Suggested answers
Students' answers can vary

Name: ____________________ Class: ____________ Date: ____________

The Oldest Winter Olympian

At 54, Scott Baird became the oldest Winter Olympian in the history of the Olympic Games when he competed with the U.S. curling team at the Torino Olympics in 2006. Baird and his team won the bronze medal and the first Olympic medal for U.S. curling.

"I'm the oldest member of the U.S. men's curling team and that's exactly one of the reasons I love curling," said Baird. "Curling is like golf, it's a lifetime sport." Baird is from Bemidji, Minnesota, which prides itself as the curling capital of the United States.

Baird has been curling since 1961. He has competed at the U.S. Men's Nationals and at the World Curling Championships. Baird said that while he taught the younger players a thing or two about the sport, he has also picked up a lot from them. "The game is always evolving and I am still learning from watching them play," said Baird. He hopes to continue playing for at least 10 more years.

Write details that support the descriptions.

A

Scott's character	Supporting details
1 passionate about the sport	
2 likes learning	
3 experienced	

B **Check [✓] the statements that show *Past*, *Present* or *Future*.**

	Past	Present	Future
1 Baird and his team won the first Olympic medal for U.S. curling.			
2 Baird is from Bemidji, Minnesota.			
3 He hopes to continue playing for at least 10 more years.			

Milo of Croton

Throughout the history of the Olympic Games there have been many famous champions. But one of the most famous and successful Olympians was also one of the most ancient. From a place in southern Italy called Croton came a strong man named Milo. Milo won the wrestling event five times. That means he was the champion for more than 20 years!

Milo competed at the 60th Olympic Games and won the Boys' Wrestling event. At the 62nd through the 66th Olympics (532–516 B.C.), he won the Men's Wrestling event. When he competed at the 67th Olympics in 512 B.C., he was defeated by a younger man. At that time, Milo must have been at least 40 years old, or perhaps even older.

Milo's strength was very famous. He trained by carrying a cow on his back up a mountain. He enjoyed showing off his strength as well. Sometimes he would hold out one hand and challenge someone to move his fingers. No one could move even his smallest finger.

However, Milo was not just a wrestler. He led the army of Croton to many victories. He was also a student of the famous Pythagoras and enjoyed poetry and art. In one legend, he protected his friends by holding up the roof when the building was falling down. He did not let go until all of his friends had gotten out safely.

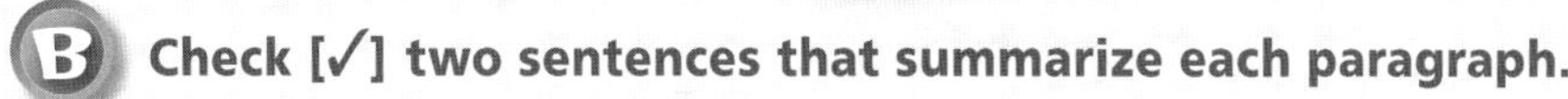

B Check [✓] two sentences that summarize each paragraph.

Paragraph 1

1 The Olympic Games and Milo of Croton are ancient. ☐
2 Milo was one of the most famous Olympic athletes. ✓
3 Milo was the Olympic wrestling champion for more than 20 years. ✓
4 There have been many famous Olympic champions. ☐

Paragraph 2

1 Milo competed in seven Olympic Games, once as a boy, six times as an adult. ✓
2 Milo won the Boy's Wrestling event. ☐
3 Milo competed in five Olympic Games, but did not win every time. ✓
4 Milo was quite old when he competed at his last Olympic Games. ☐

C Write details from the passage that support the descriptions.

Milo's character	Supporting details
1 determined to win every time	won the wrestling event at the ancient Olympic Games five times
2 enjoyed competing at a young age	won the Boys' Wrestling event at the 60th Olympic Games
3 loyal to friends	held up the roof of the building until his friends had gotten out safely
4 liked attention	enjoyed showing off his strength

Unit 9 Historic Cities

Unit Overview

SUBJECT	History/Culture and People
READING SKILL	Understanding paragraph development
TEXT TYPE	Content-based passage

Reading Skill

Understanding paragraph development

Passages are developed using well-ordered paragraphs. Knowing how paragraphs are built helps you better understand a reading. Every sentence should build on the one before it. Each sentence should have a flow or connection to the next sentence, as should each paragraph to the next.

For example, if you are writing a paragraph about the beginning of a city, you should start off with information that is basic and you can build on.

The city was founded in 1875. It is over 100 years old. There are more than one million people living there now.

In the example, notice how the first sentence is related to the next one, and so on. The second and third sentences build on the information presented in the first sentence.

As an activity, find a well-ordered paragraph from a magazine, brochure, etc., and cut it up into individual sentences. Have students work in groups to put the paragraph back together.

Answers for Unit 9 Worksheet (p. 69)

A

1. Cross-scan for: founded — Answer: Shiva.
2. Cross-scan for: writer — Answer: Mark Twain.
3. Cross-scan for: population — Answer: About 1.3 million people.
4. Cross-scan for: river — Answer: The Ganges.

B

1. B 2. D 3. A 4. C

Historic Cities

Unit 9

A What do you know about your city's history? Discuss your answers.

Reading Skill

Understanding paragraph development

Passages are developed using well-ordered paragraphs. Knowing how paragraphs are built helps you better understand a reading.

B Number the sentences in the correct order.

3 A When adults played, it was quite dangerous. 2 B They had courts for ceremonial ball games. 4 C Children played a safer version for fun. 1 D The Maya also knew how to have fun.

25 **Read the passage.**

The Mighty Maya

The Maya in central America is one of the world's most well-known ancient civilizations. Its classical period lasted between the years A.D. 250 and 900. (A)

Though far from Europe, the Maya civilization had a lot in common with Greece and Egypt. (B) Just like the Greeks, the Maya had stone buildings and they worshipped gods. They also had many independent city-states similar to those of ancient Greece. Like the Egyptians, the Maya built very tall pyramids. (C)

The Maya achieved a lot of things that were unique to their civilization. Some of their cities were very large. The city of Tikal had 100,000 to 200,000 people. (D) The Maya also invented things like rubber balls and shoes. (E) They were very good at mathematics and astronomy.

The Maya also knew how to have fun. They had courts for ceremonial ball games. (F) When adults played, it was quite dangerous. (G) Children played a safer version for fun.

(H) The Maya civilization started to decline after A.D. 900, but we can still visit their old sites and cities. Even after thousands of years, the Maya achievements are still impressive.

Answer the questions.

1 How long did the Maya classical period last? 650 years.

2 How were the Maya similar to the Egyptians? They also built very tall pyramids.

3 What did the Maya invent? Rubber balls and shoes.

Practice

Insert each sentence into the passage. Write the letter.

1	Some of the similarities between these civilizations were quite amazing.	B
2	They were quite good thinkers.	E
3	Almost every Maya city had at least one of these ball courts.	F
4	This was a period of more than 600 years.	A
5	The Maya pyramids had temple rooms at the top, but had the same steep sides and steps as the Egyptian ones.	C
6	Of course, even great civilizations start to break down as time goes by.	H
7	That is as big as some of today's modern cities.	D
8	Pictures show adult players bleeding from injuries.	G

TIP When you come to a circled letter in the passage, scan the sentences above and decide which sentence builds on the information given in the passage.

Look at the highlighted words in the passage. Find out what they mean using the Mini-dictionary on pages 69–72.

Integration

G 26 **Listen and complete the paragraph.**

The ancient Maya (1) played ball games not just for fun but as a religious activity. The ball games were played in (2) courts of different sizes, with some sized 166 meters long and 68 meters (3) wide. (A) At either end of the court, there was a stone ring on the wall. The players passed a large rubber ball through the ring to score a goal. (B) The game was (4) dangerous because of the stone walls and players hitting each other. (C) However, losing the (5) game was even more dangerous! (D)

H **Insert each sentence into the paragraph above. Write the letter.**

1. The first team to do this was the winner. B
2. Sometimes, the losing team was killed as a sacrifice to the gods. D
3. The courts were shaped like a capital "I" and had stone walls and ramps. A
4. For this reason, players wore special padding to protect themselves. C

I **What is your favorite ball game? Tell the class.**

Name: ______________________ Class: ______________ Date: ______________

The Ancient City of Varanasi

Varanasi, also known as Benaras, is a famous Indian city situated on the banks of the river Ganges in the north. It is one of the oldest cities in the world, dating back thousands of years. (A)

Many famous people have visited Varanasi over the years. (B) American writer Mark Twain once wrote, "Benaras is older than history, older than tradition, older even than legend, and looks twice as old as all of them put together!"

According to myths, Varanasi was founded by the Hindu god Shiva, making it one of the most important places for Hindus. (C) Varanasi is strongly linked with the river Ganges. Hindus believe that bathing in the river will get rid of all their worries and sins.

Varanasi has a population of about 1.3 million people. (D) It has several small industries, including silk- and sari-making, textiles and handicrafts.

(A) Write the best key words or phrases to cross-scan for. Then cross-scan the passage and write the answers.

1 Which Hindu god is said to have founded Varanasi?

Cross-scan for: ______________ Answer: ______________

2 Which famous writer wrote about Varanasi?

Cross-scan for: ______________ Answer: ______________

3 What is the population of Varanasi?

Cross-scan for: ______________ Answer: ______________

4 Which river is Varanasi linked with?

Cross-scan for: ______________ Answer: ______________

(B) Insert each sentence into the passage. Write the letter.

1 They were very interested in the city's history. ☐

2 Its population has gone up and down over the years. ☐

3 People often refer to it as a city of temples and learning. ☐

4 More than one million Hindus visit the city each year. ☐

Unit 10 Follow the sign!

Unit Overview

SUBJECT	Social Studies
READING SKILL	Understanding signs
TEXT TYPE	Sign

Reading Skill

Understanding signs

Signs help you in many different ways. They give directions, rules, or information on places, events, prices and times. They give information through very simple and short statements, as well as visual aids. Most signs have fewer than five words on them. Visual signs are usually easier to understand.

Download some common visual signs from the Internet (include humorous ones as well). Then give each student a sheet showing these signs. Get them to write down what the signs mean. Discuss them with students.

Another activity is to say a statement like *I'm hungry and want to eat cheap pizza.* and have students create a sign for this. Make up other statements and get them to create signs for them.

Answers for Unit 10 Worksheet (p. 75)

1. F
2. B
3. D
4. C
5. E
6. A

A What would you do if you got lost in a new place? Discuss your answers.

Reading Skill

Understanding signs

Signs help you in many different ways. They give directions, rules, or information on places, events, prices and times.

B What information do these signs give? Write your answers.

1

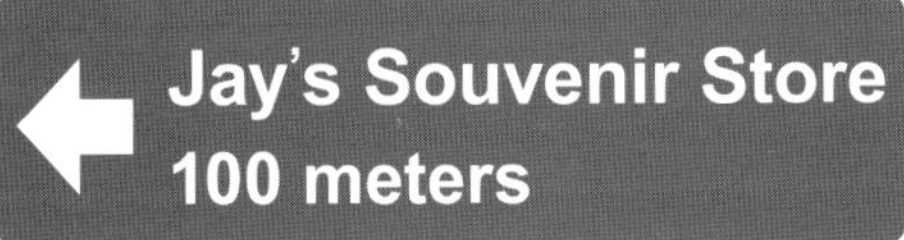

directions to the souvenir store

2

eating and drinking are not allowed

Reading

27 Read about Chichen Itza and look at the signs.

D Answer the questions.

1 Which sign tells us where we can buy food? Sign "H."

2 What time does the Chichen Itza site close? 5.30 p.m.

3 What are the warrior statues made of? Stone.

E Choose the correct sign for each statement. Write the letter.

1	Buses park to the left, cars park to the right.	G
2	Turn left if you want to eat Maya food. Turn right for snacks and drinks.	H
3	Do not leave trash on the ground.	C
4	Go there if you want to buy something to remember your trip by.	A
5	It is an old building built on top of an older building.	J
6	This is how much it costs to get in.	I
7	These are the directions to three famous places in the site.	D
8	It is a building for soldiers.	F
9	This unique building was where the Maya people watched the sky.	B
10	Buy your tickets first and then meet here to start the tour.	E

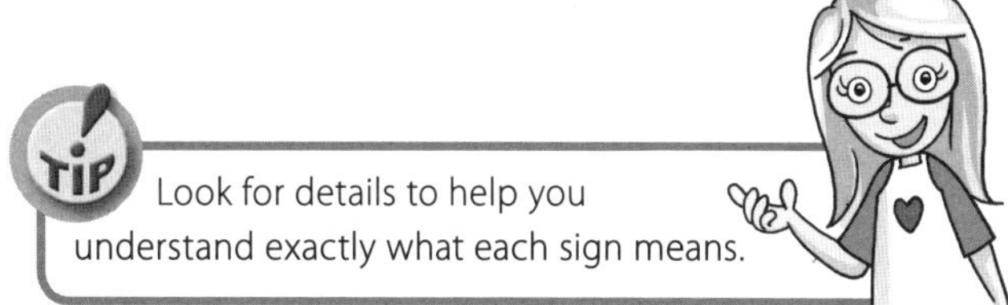

F Look at the highlighted words in the reading. Find out what they mean using the Mini-dictionary on pages 69–72.

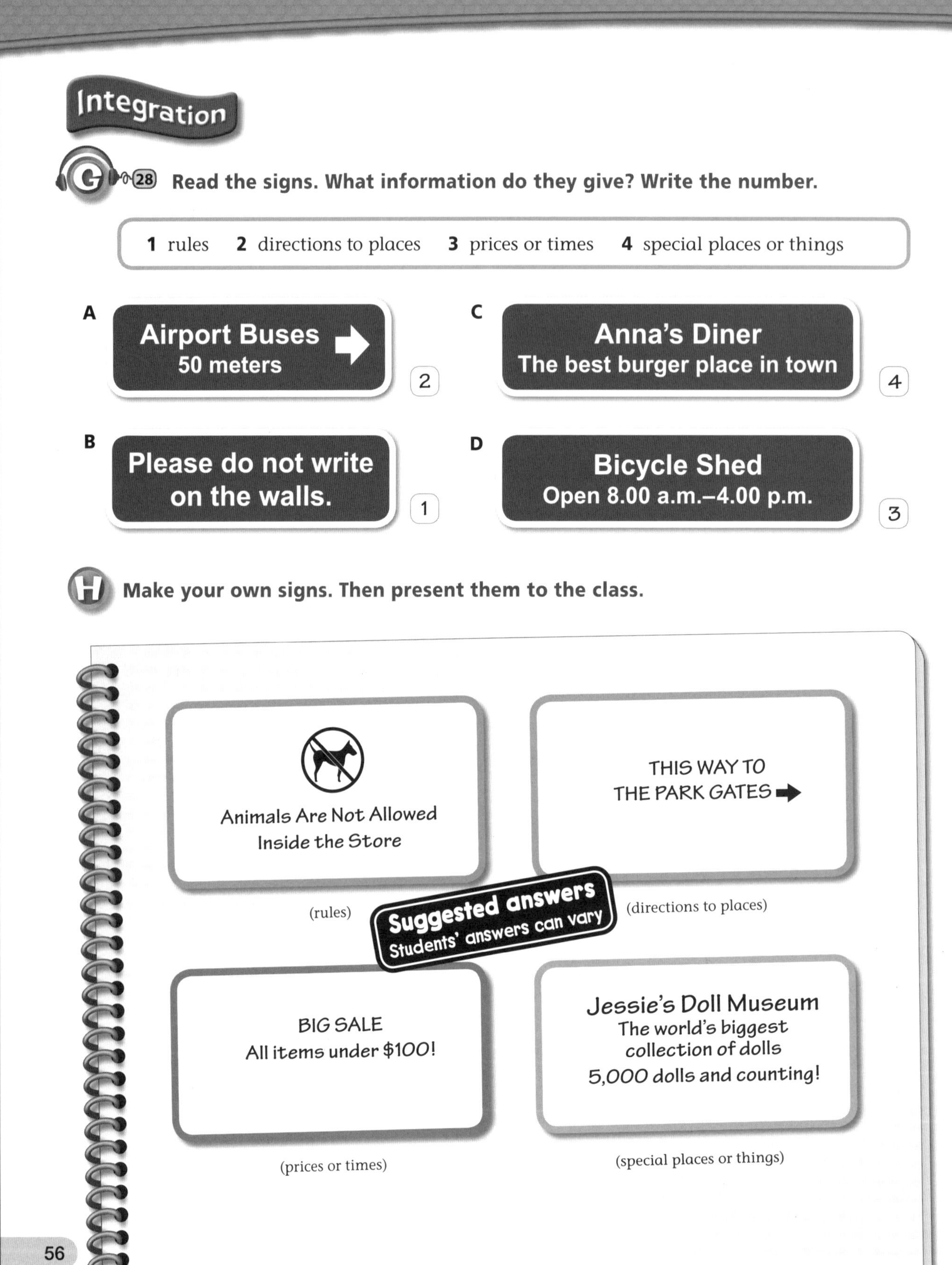
Integration
G 28 Read the signs. What information do they give? Write the number.
1 rules 2 directions to places 3 prices or times 4 special places or things
A
Airport Buses
50 meters
2
C
Anna's Diner
The best burger place in town
4
B
Please do not write on the walls.
1
D
Bicycle Shed
Open 8.00 a.m.–4.00 p.m.
3
H Make your own signs. Then present them to the class.
Animals Are Not Allowed
Inside the Store
(rules)
THIS WAY TO
THE PARK GATES
(directions to places)
Suggested answers
Students' answers can vary
BIG SALE
All items under $100!
(prices or times)
Jessie's Doll Museum
The world's biggest
collection of dolls
5,000 dolls and counting!
(special places or things)
56

Name: ______________________ Class: ______________ Date: ______________

A

Park buses only in red zones

Park cars in yellow zones

B

No littering in the park

C

The Banla River 500 m ⇨

⇦ The City Center 300 m

D

Beware of pickpockets

E

GUIDED TOURS

Adults: $5

Students: $3

Children under 5 are free of charge

F

Food and drinks are not allowed in temples

Choose the correct sign for each statement. Write the letter.

1. Don't drink or eat in the temple. ☐
2. Do not drop trash in the park. ☐
3. Keep your wallet and money safe from thieves. ☐
4. The river and the city center are in opposite directions. ☐
5. This is how much a guided tour costs. ☐
6. Park in the correct zone. ☐

Read the passage.

The Maya Society

Kings were very important to the Maya. Without a king, kingdoms would fall and disappear. The greater a king was, the more people came to live in his city. (A)

The Maya were very good artists. The art that they made on pottery, stones and temple walls is often said to be the most beautiful in ancient America.

(B) The writing system of the Maya is one of the oldest in the Americas. At present, there are almost 10,000 examples of Maya writing. The Maya wrote on walls, pottery, monuments and even tree bark. They used red and black ink in a lot of their writing. (C)

B Check [✓] two sentences that summarize the third paragraph.

1 There are thousands of examples of ancient Maya writing. [✓]

2 The ancient Maya liked to write on tree barks. [ ]

3 Ancient Maya writing was found on monuments. [ ]

4 The Maya wrote on anything, using a lot of red and black ink. [✓]

C Insert each sentence into the passage above. Write the letter.

1 This caused neighboring kingdoms to call the Maya cities the "land of black and red." [C]

2 The importance of kings makes the Maya civilization similar to many other civilizations. [A]

3 Another interesting thing about the Maya was their writing. [B]

Review 5

D **Read the signs. Then choose the correct sign for each statement. Write the letter.**

A

Jail
This strong stone building had wooden bars across the windows and doors.

C

Guided Tours
2 hours: $12
Half day: $18
Full day: $24

B

Exit
Information
Kiosk

D

Do not climb the sides of the pyramid

1 A tour guide can show you around the site for a few hours, half a day or the whole day. C

2 Walking on the pyramid can be dangerous, so please do not do that. D

3 Go straight ahead if you want to leave. Turn right if you want drinks or snacks. Turn left if you want to ask for information. B

4 It is a place for people who did bad things. A

E **Which signs give the following information? Write the letter.**

1 directions to places B

2 rules D

3 special places or things A

4 prices or times C

Unit 11

Watch what you eat!

Unit Overview

SUBJECT	Science and Nature
READING SKILL	Finding information from graphs
TEXT TYPE	Content-based passage

Reading Skill

Finding information from graphs

Like tables, graphs show you detailed information quickly and clearly. A graph has a horizontal axis and a vertical axis. At their most basic level, one axis will represent items being compared and the other will show the values they are compared by. Sometimes a graph has two or more colors. What the colors represent will be indicated in a color key next to the graph. Above or below the graph is the title, which gives a general idea of what the graph is all about.

Draw or copy a graph onto the board. Get students to look closely at it and tell you what the graph shows. Ask them questions and have them find the answers from the graph. Help students to study the graph and not get confused by what the axes stand for.

A good online activity is to have students go to the U.S. Department of Agriculture's website and complete their own My Pyramid Plan. They should then make their own graph based on the information in the plan and compare it to other students' graphs. Help them write the title as well as other information such as servings and food groups.

Answers for Unit 11 Worksheet (p. 83)

1. Boys.
2. Less.
3. Six servings.
4. Grains.

Watch what you eat!

A What kinds of food do you eat every day? Discuss your answers.

Reading Skill

Finding information from graphs

Like tables, graphs show you detailed information quickly and clearly.

B Identify the information in the graph. Write the letter.

A the minimum (smallest) amount of vegetables we should eat daily

B the maximum (largest) amount of grain we should eat daily

C the food we should eat more of

D the minimum amount of grain we should eat daily

E the maximum amount of vegetables we should eat daily

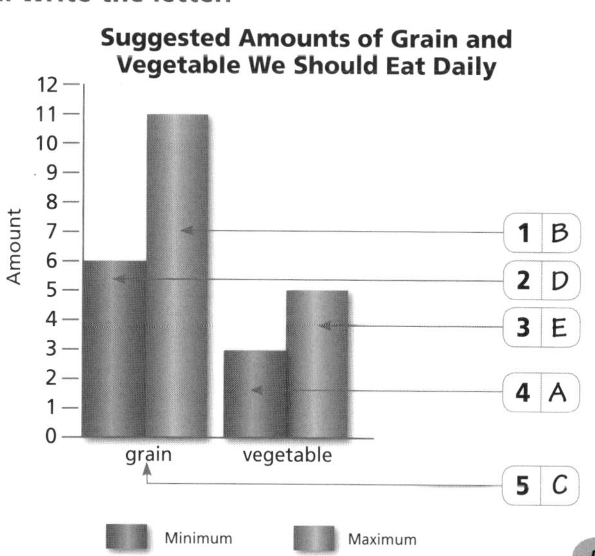

Read the passage.

How to Eat Healthy

Food is a basic part of living and growing. It gives your body the energy it needs to work. It also gives your body important nutrients—the things that help your body grow and become stronger. You need different kinds of nutrients, such as carbohydrates, fats, vitamins, minerals and proteins.

Your body gets carbohydrates from foods like cereal, bread, pasta, rice, fruit and vegetables. Your body gets fats from margarine, butter and sweets. Vitamins and minerals can be found in foods like eggs, meat, nuts, soy beans, bananas or even table salt. Proteins are found in dairy products like milk, cheese and yogurt but also in meat, fish, eggs and beans.

However, you do not need all the nutrients in the same amounts. Your body needs a lot of carbohydrates but not too much fat. To have a balanced diet, it will be useful to find out how many servings of each food you need every day.

What counts as one serving?

Grain
- 1 slice of bread
- 1 ounce of cereal
- ½ cup of cooked cereal, rice or pasta

Vegetable
- 1 cup of raw leafy vegetables
- ½ cup of other vegetables—cooked or chopped raw
- ¾ cup of vegetable juice

Fruit
- 1 medium apple, banana or orange
- ½ cup of chopped, cooked or canned fruit
- ¾ cup of fruit juice

Dairy
- 1 cup of milk or yogurt
- 1 ½ ounces of natural cheese
- 2 ounces of processed cheese

Meat, fish and egg
- 2–3 ounces of cooked lean meat, poultry or fish
- ½ cup of cooked dry beans or 1 egg counts as 1 ounce of lean meat.
- 2 tablespoons of peanut butter or ⅓ cup of nuts counts as 1 ounce of meat.

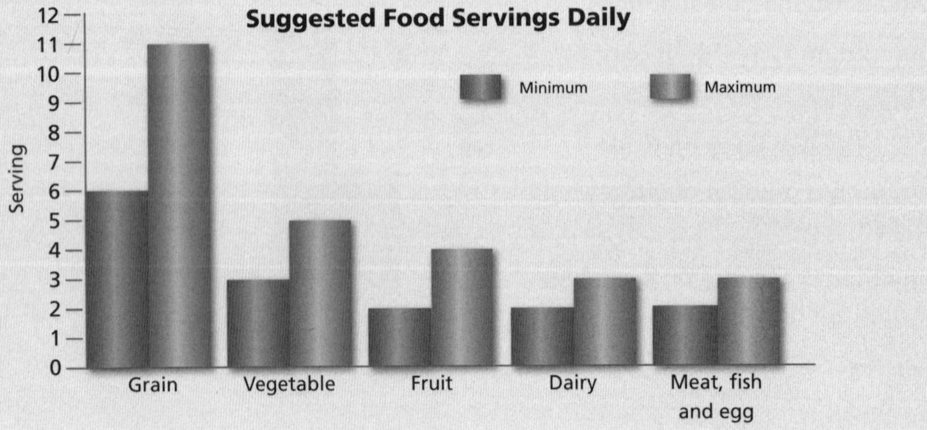

D Answer the questions.

1 What are nutrients? Things that help the body grow and become stronger.

2 What are examples of dairy products? Milk, cheese and yogurt.

3 Which do we need more of, carbohydrates or fats? Carbohydrates.

Practice

E Look at the graph and write the answers.

1	Which color on the graph shows the maximum food servings?	Blue.
2	What is the minimum serving of fruit we should have every day?	2.
3	What is the maximum serving of dairy products we should have every day?	3.
4	Would eight servings of cereal, rice or pasta every day be OK?	Yes.
5	Add the minimum servings of fruit and vegetables. How many servings are there altogether?	5.
6	Which should we eat more of, meat or vegetables?	Vegetables.

F Look at the highlighted words in the passage. Find out what they mean using the Mini-dictionary on pages 69–72.

Integration

G **Write what you and three classmates usually eat.**

Name	Breakfast	Lunch	Dinner
1 Me	cereal with milk	vegetable salad with grilled chicken; mushroom soup	spaghetti with meatballs
2 Bob	2 slices of bread, with 2 tablespoons of peanut butter	1 cup of noodles with vegetables and fish balls; 1 glass of watermelon juice	fried chicken with 2 cups of rice
3 Jane	apple; yogurt	ham and cheese sandwich; fruit salad	roast beef with 1 cup of rice
4 Tim	2 slices of toasted bread, with ham and egg	hamburger; soft drink	steak; French fries

Suggested answers
Students' answers can vary

H **Make a graph for one of your classmates using the information above. Then present it to the class.**

Student's name: Bob

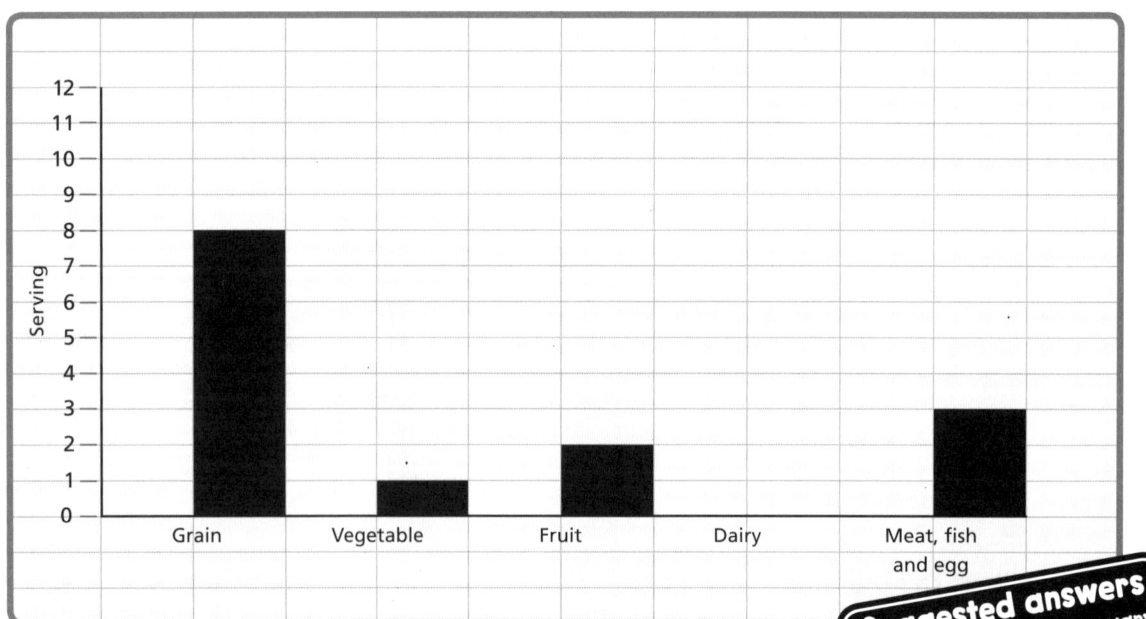

Suggested answers
Students' answers can vary

Name: ______________________ Class: ______________ Date: ______________

Changes to the Food Guide

The U.S. Department of Agriculture (USDA) has revised the Food Guide Pyramid. The new guide factors in a person's age, gender and level of activity. It shows how important it is to exercise and be active every day, while eating the right amount of food. People who are more active burn more calories, so they can eat more.

The table below shows the suggested daily food servings for boys and girls aged 9 to 13 who do less than 30 minutes of activity daily.

Suggested Food Servings Daily
For 9–13-year-olds

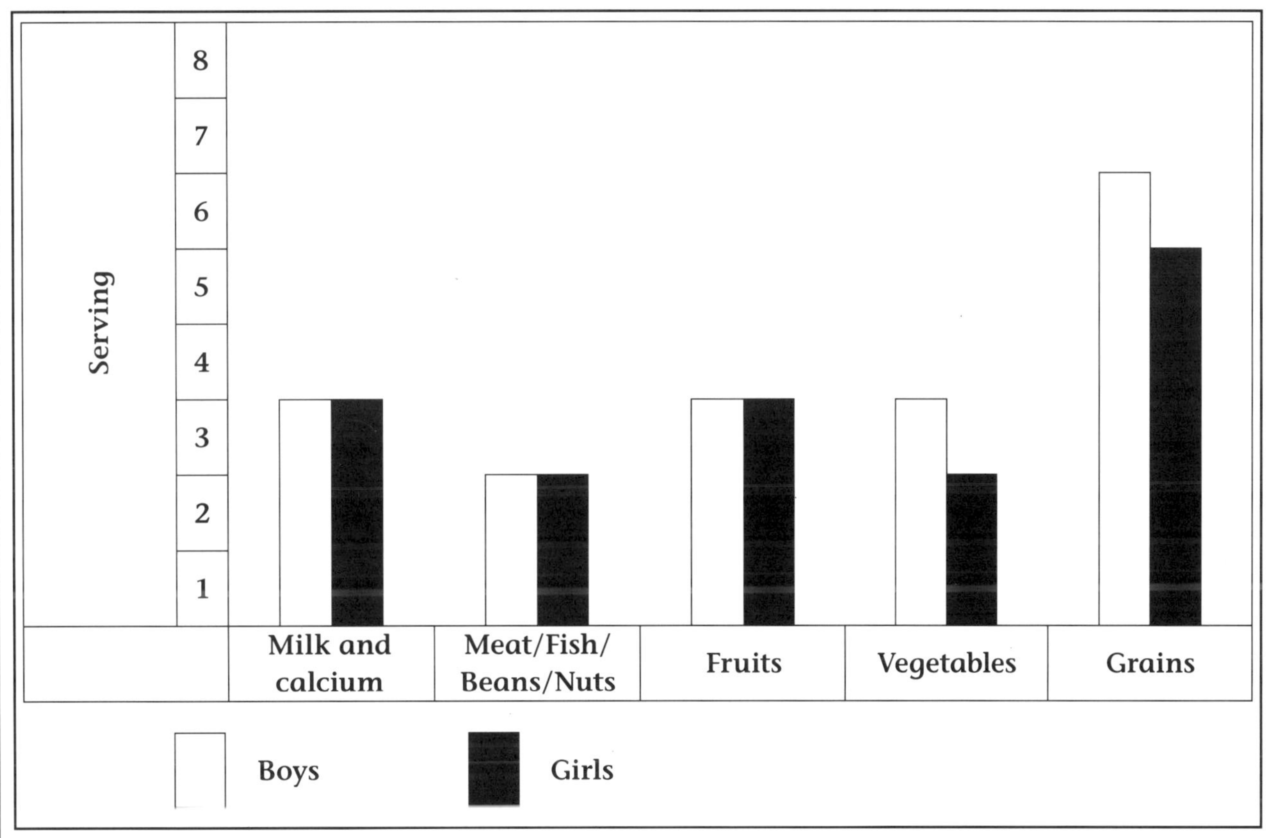

Look at the graph and write the answers.

1. Who should eat more vegetables, boys or girls? ______________
2. Should girls eat more or less grain than boys? ______________
3. How many servings of fruit and vegetable should boys eat daily? ______________
4. Which should boys and girls eat more of, vegetables or grains? ______________

Unit 12 Out at the Diner

Unit Overview

SUBJECT	Science and Nature
READING SKILL	Understanding menus
TEXT TYPE	Menu

Reading Skill

Understanding menus

A menu lists the different foods and drinks that are available in a restaurant. It tells you what they are made from, how much they cost and how big the servings are. Some menus have little icons that indicate which foods are healthy, spicy, for kids, low-fat, for diabetics, etc.

On most menus, dishes are listed according to the times they are served. Breakfast is the first thing on menus, followed by lunch, dinner and then desserts and drinks.

Collect menus from different restaurants and bring them to class (places that offer delivery service will usually supply menus). Have students look at the menus, and then have them make their own menus. Their menus should have 10 items, each with a name, description, price, etc. Have them share their menus with their classmates and then pretend to order what they would like.

Answers for Unit 12 Worksheet (p. 89)

1. Cheeseburger and large Juice, $4.64
2. Caesar Salad, Hamburger and small Iced Tea, $9.85
3. Tomato Soup, Caesar Salad and Large Fries, $9.75

[Suggested answers; students' answers can vary]

Out at the Diner

A What do you usually order when eating out? Discuss your answers.

Reading Skill

Understanding menus

A menu lists the different foods and drinks that are available in a restaurant. It tells you what they are made from, how much they cost and how big the servings are.

B Check [✓] the information you can identify.

Tony's Diner
It's good for you!

Breakfast (all day from 6:00 a.m.)	Regular	Large
White Rice with Mixed Vegetables * *With or without egg topping*	$2.89	$4.49
Granola Cereal with Fresh Fruit *With or without milk*	$1.89	$3.49
Fruit Smoothie * *Papaya, strawberry or celery*	$1.49	$2.49

Note: Items marked * can be delivered between 3:00 p.m. and 9:00 p.m. daily, but only as large orders.

- meals offered [✓]
- time that drinks are served [ ]
- meal servings [✓]
- prices [✓]
- delivery service [✓]

32 **Read the menu.**

Tony's Diner

It's good for you!

	Regular	Large
Breakfast (all day from 6:00 a.m.)		
White Rice with Mixed Vegetables * *With or without egg topping*	$2.89	$4.49
Granola Cereal with Fresh Fruit *With or without milk*	$1.89	$3.49
Fruit Smoothie * *Papaya, strawberry or celery*	$1.49	$2.49
Lunch (from 11:30 a.m.)		
Sandwich on a Stick * *Whole grain bread with vegetable and meat*	$4.25	$7.45
Pasta Perfect *Pasta with wild mushrooms*	$5.25	$8.45
Fruit Salad *A platter of seven different fruits*	$4.25	$7.35
Dinner (from 5:30 p.m.)		
Veggie Burger *Grilled vegetable burger on a bun*	$3.29	$4.59
Stuffed Bread * *Bread with chicken and avocado filling*	$3.45	$5.49
Steak Surprise *Grilled steak with vegetable and baked potato*	$5.75	$9.85
Juice (orange, apple, grape, lime, watermelon)	$1.99	

Note: Items marked * can be delivered between 3:00 p.m. and 9:00 p.m. daily, but only as large orders.

D Answer the questions.

1 How much does a large order of granola cereal cost? $3.49.

2 What is in the Stuffed Bread? Chicken and avocado.

3 How many meals are available for delivery? Four.

Practice

E Write the name of the meal and the serving size for each person.

1 It is 2:00 p.m. Frank likes bread. He is hungry and he can eat a lot.
Sandwich on a Stick, large

2 It is 7:00 a.m. Rebecca wants something with egg, but she is not very hungry.
White Rice with Mixed Vegetables, with egg topping, regular

3 It is 7:30 a.m. Thomas really likes fruit but he does not like milk. He is very hungry.
Granola Cereal with Fresh Fruit, without milk, large

4 It is 8:00 p.m. Karly really likes steak but she is not very hungry.
Steak Surprise, regular

5 It is 5:00 p.m. Peter is very hungry. He wants to eat something with mushrooms.
Pasta Perfect, large

F Look at the highlighted words in the menu. Find out what they mean using the Mini-dictionary on pages 69–72.

Integration

G Write a healthy menu for a new diner.

Dylan's Delight
(name of diner)

	Regular	Large
Breakfast (from 7:30 a.m. **to** 11:30 a.m.**)**		
• Cereal Bowl	$ 1.75	$ 2.35
Granola cereal with melon and almonds		
• Yummy Yogurt	$ 1.55	$ 1.85
Low-fat yogurt with peach and strawberries		
Lunch (from 11:30 a.m. **to** 6:00 p.m.**)**		
• Super Salad	$ 2.45	$ 3.25
Green vegetables with avocado and beef		
• Meat in Lettuce	$ 2.55	$ 3.35
Chicken salad in a large lettuce leaf		
Dinner (from 6:00 p.m**)**		
• Chicken Spaghetti	$ 2.89	$ 3.75
Spaghetti with chicken grilled in cinnamon		
• Stuffed Cabbage	$ 2.45	$ 3.25
Cabbage stuffed with beef or turkey		

Drinks

• Apple Juice	$ 1.45	• Lime Soda	$ 1.35
• Cranberry Juice	$ 1.65	• Green Tea	$ 1.55

Suggested answers
Students' answers can vary

Exchange menus with a classmate. Ask and answer.

What would you like?

I would like a large order of spaghetti and an apple juice, please.

Name: ____________________ Class: ____________ Date: ____________

Jack's Sandwich Shop
Open from 11 a.m.–11 p.m.

Side Dishes

Chicken Soup $3.85
Tomato Soup $2.25
Caesar Salad $5.75

Sandwiches

Hamburger $2.45
Double Hamburger $3.49
Cheeseburger $2.65
Double Cheeseburger $3.85

All burgers are served with lettuce, onion, tomato and pickles.

Small Fries $1.35
Large Fries $1.75

Soft Drinks, Juice & Iced Tea

Small $1.65
Large $1.99

Write the name of the meal, the serving size and the cost for each person.

1. Billy wants to eat something with cheese. He loves fruit drinks. He is not very hungry.

   ____

2. Lucy wants something healthy for a side dish. She also wants a hamburger and an iced tea.

   ____

3. Lizzy is hungry. She loves soup and vegetables.

   ____

A 33 **Read the passage.**

Going Easy on Snacks and Fast Food

Fats are common in the food we eat. In the right amount, they are good for us. (A) They give us energy and protect our bodies from cold weather. However, not all kinds of fats are good for us. (B) One unhealthy kind of fat is called trans fat. Trans fat can cause serious heart problems, but it is used in many foods because it helps the food keep its flavor longer. Trans fats are common in snacks or fast food. (C) If we eat a lot of these foods, we are putting our health in danger.

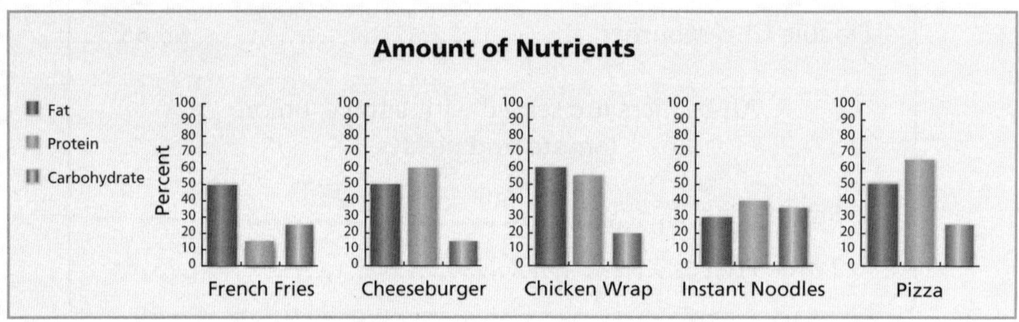

B **Insert the sentence into the paragraph above. Write the letter.**

Snacks and fast food are often high in fat and we need to be careful how much of these foods we eat every day. C

C **Look at the graph and write the answers.**

1 What color shows fat content? Red.

2 How much protein does a cheeseburger have? 60 percent.

3 What do the graphs show about the fat content in snacks and fast food?

The graphs show that snacks and fast food have a lot of fat.

34 **Read the menu.**

Helen's Heaven

Lunch (from 11:00 a.m.)

	Regular	Large
Seafood Pasta Spaghetti with mussels and tomato sauce	$4.25	$7.45
Yellow and Green Salad Fresh lettuce with orange slices	$3.25	$6.35

Dinner (from 5:30 p.m.)

	Regular	Large
Salmon Plate Smoked salmon with mushrooms, lettuce, string beans and tomatoes	$5.25	$7.45
Beef Roast Roasted beef with grilled red onions and avocado	$5.99	$8.25

Write the name of the meal and the serving size for each of your friends.

1 It is 7:00 p.m. Your friend likes beef. She is not very hungry.

Beef Roast, regular

2 It is 11:30 a.m. Your friend loves spaghetti and he is very hungry.

Seafood Pasta, large

68

Mini-dictionary

*Note: The page numbers here refer to the **Student Book**.*

A

accompany	*v*	to go with another person or other people	p. 34
admission	*n*	the price to go into a building or participate in an event	p. 54
amazing	*adj*	surprising; fantastic	p. 14
argue	*v*	to give reasons for or against	p. 24
asteroid	*n*	any of the large objects between Mars and Jupiter	p. 24
astronomer	*n*	a scientist who studies space, stars and planets	p. 24
astronomy	*n*	the study of space, stars and planets	p. 50
attempt	*n*	tries; acts of trying	p. 20

B

bachelor's degree	*n*	a qualification given to a person who has finished university	p. 44
balanced diet	*n*	regular eating of the right foods in the right amount	p. 60
ban	*v*	to say that something must not be done	p. 44
bronze	*adj*	a kind of red-brown metal	p. 40

C

carbohydrate	*n*	food (usually made from plants) with carbon, hydrogen or oxygen	p. 60
ceremonial	*adj*	part of a special event	p. 50
certificate	*n*	a special document showing something is true or has been done	p. 34
chatter	*v*	to talk fast without stopping, especially about unimportant things	p. 14
civilization	*n*	a society that is well-organized and developed	p. 50
classical period	*n*	time of great art and success	p. 50
classify	*v*	to put in a special group	p. 24
clear	*v*	to jump over something without touching it	p. 44
communicate	*v*	to talk or send messages	p. 34
compete	*v*	to take part in a contest	p. 40
complete	*adj*	having all the necessary parts; whole; full	p. 10
condition	*n*	the state that something is in	p. 20
continent	*n*	a large area of land surrounded by sea	p. 30
criteria	*n*	standards on which a decision may be based	p. 24
crown	*n*	something circular and decorative worn on the head to show victory or honor	p. 40
culture	*n*	the way people live and their beliefs	p. 30

D

decline	*v*	to go down in level or importance; to become smaller or weaker	p. 50
demand	*v*	to ask for or command strongly	p. 14
depart	*v*	to leave	p. 34
disappear	*v*	to become impossible to see or find; to vanish	p. 10
disaster	*n*	a sudden bad end or failure	p. 20
discovery	*n*	the act of finding	p. 24
distant	*adj*	far away; not close	p. 24
dwarf	*adj*	smaller than the normal size	p. 24

E

echo	*v*	to make a sound that repeats	p. 14
encourage	*v*	to say or do something that helps someone take action	p. 44
energy	*n*	the power or strength to do work	p. 60
exist	*v*	to be: to be real	p. 20
explore	*v*	to travel through or look at something carefully to find out what is there or what it is like	p. 20

F

filling	*n*	a food mixture that is put inside a pie, sandwich or other types of food	p. 64

G

gasp	*v*	to make a quick breathing sound	p. 14
granola cereal	*n*	breakfast food made from grains, fruits and nuts	p. 64
grilled	*adj*	cooked over direct heat, using a grill	p. 64
guided tour	*n*	a trip led by someone who tells interesting information about the place	p. 54
gymnastics	*n*	a sport in which a person does exercises on metal bars to show strength, balance and body control	p. 44

H

harbour (british english) **harbor** (american english)	*n*	water along the coast where ships can go safely	p. 34
harness	*n*	strong material that is put around a person to stop them from falling	p. 34

I

icy	*adj*	very cold	p. 24
impossible	*adj*	not possible; cannot be done	p. 10
impressive	*adj*	amazing; admirable	p. 50
include	*v*	to have; to contain; to be part of	p. 34
independent	*adj*	not ruled or controlled by others	p. 50
intercontinental	*adj*	going from one continent to another	p. 30
international date line	*n*	an invisible line that separates each calendar day from the next (the date to the east of the line is one day later than the west)	p. 30
involve	*v*	to include; to have	p. 40

K

kingdom	*n*	a country with a king or queen as the ruler	p. 40
kiosk	*n*	a small structure, with one or more open sides, that is used for selling things	p. 54

L

lean	*v*	to move or bend the body in a particular direction	p. 14
litter	*n*	trash like cans or food wrappers that are left on the ground	p. 54

M

margarine	*n*	food made from vegetable oils and skim milk	p. 60
maximum	*n*	the largest number or amount that is possible or allowed	p. 34
measure	*v*	to find out the size or amount	p. 20
mineral	*n*	natural substance found usually in water or the ground	p. 60
mission	*n*	a flight operation of a spacecraft or an aircraft	p. 20
modern	*adj*	of recent time or the present	p. 40
mushroom	*n*	a kind of fungus that has a stem and a wide top, some of which can be eaten	p. 64

N

narrow	*adj*	not wide; very thin	p. 30
notice	*n*	information or warning that something is going to change or happen	p. 34
numb	*adj*	unable to think or feel in a certain way	p. 14

O

observatory	*n*	a building from which people watch the sky, stars and planets	p. 54
opposite	*n*	something that is as different as possible from another	p. 10
orbit	*n*	a path traveled by an object that is circling a much larger object	p. 24
organize	*v*	to make the necessary arrangements so that an activity can happen	p. 40

P

panic	*v*	to suddenly become very worried and scared	p. 14
participant	*n*	a person who takes part in an activity or event	p. 40
pasta	*n*	food made from flour, eggs and water, and cut into different shapes	p. 64
perform	*v*	to do something skillful in front of an audience	p. 10
platter	*n*	a large plate used for serving food	p. 64
pole vault	*n*	the sport of jumping over a high bar using a long pole	p. 44
preserved	*adj*	kept in good condition; protected from damage	p. 54
produce	*v*	to make; to create	p. 10
promote	*v*	to make something popular	p. 40
protein	*n*	natural substance made from amino acids	p. 60
puff	*n*	a small cloud	p. 10
pyramid	*n*	a stone structure with a square base and four triangular sides that go up to a point at the top	p. 50

R

Word	Part of speech	Definition	Page
rank	*n*	the position, grade or title in an organization	p. 44
recent	*adj*	not long ago	p. 20
restore	*v*	to bring or put something back to the way it was before	p. 10
ruin	*n*	the part of a building that is left after the rest has been destroyed	p. 54

S

Word	Part of speech	Definition	Page
separate	*v*	to keep apart; to make a distance between	p. 30
serving	*n*	an amount of food eaten at one time	p. 60
smoothie	*n*	a creamy drink made of fruit or vegetable blended with juice, milk or yogurt	p. 64
snap	*v*	to make a short sharp sound	p. 10
souvenir	*adj*	for or relating to a souvenir—something that a person keeps to remember a place	p. 54
soy bean	*n*	seed of an Asian plant from which oil and food are made	p. 60
stare	*v*	to look hard and long	p. 14
statue	*n*	a stone or metal decoration made to look like a person	p. 40
steak	*n*	a large thick piece of meat, usually beef	p. 64
strait	*n*	a narrow passage of water that connects larger seas	p. 30
streetcar	*n*	a vehicle (like a small train) that moves on rails and carries passengers	p. 44
successful	*adj*	having the intended effect or result	p. 20
surface	*n*	the top or outside layer	p. 20
sweets	*n*	foods containing a lot of sugar	p. 60

T

Word	Part of speech	Definition	Page
temple	*n*	a special building where people worship gods	p. 54
throne	*n*	a special chair for a king or queen	p. 54
topping	*n*	food put on top of another food to make it look nicer or taste better	p. 64
trade	*n*	the business of buying and selling	p. 30
twilight	*adj*	relating to the the time when day is starting to become night	p. 34

U

Word	Part of speech	Definition	Page
unique	*adj*	special; one of a kind	p. 50
usable	*adj*	can work and be used	p. 30

V

Word	Part of speech	Definition	Page
vitamin	*n*	natural substance important for good health	p. 60

W

Word	Part of speech	Definition	Page
wand	*n*	a small stick used for doing magic tricks	p. 10
whole grain bread	*n*	bread that uses all of the grain, including the outer layer	p. 64
wink	*v*	to close and open one eye very quickly	p. 14
withstand	*v*	to resist or stand against; to stay strong or unharmed	p. 30
world record	*n*	the best performance or achievement in the world	p. 44
worried	*adj*	uneasy or troubled about something	p. 44
worship	*v*	to show respect and love for a god by praying	p. 50

CD Script

Unit 1 Student Book p. 12

Listen and write the names of the magic tricks.

Magic Mark is a young magician with very special acts in his show. For his teleportation trick, Mark puts two cages next to each other. He locks himself in one of the cages and both cages fill up with smoke. When the smoke clears, Mark is suddenly in the other cage! This trick is called "The Great Cage Swap."

For his penetration trick, Mark takes an item and puts it through a card, without ripping it. He puts a pen, a ruler and even scissors through the card! This trick is called "Through the card."

For his levitation trick, Mark takes a woman from the audience and asks her to lie down on a table. He says some magic words and the woman's body starts to rise! Mark passes hoops over the woman to show that there are no wires holding her up. This trick is called "Ladyfloat."

Mark's show is a real treat for the audience!

Unit 4 Student Book p. 26

Listen and complete the table.

Did you know that Jupiter is the biggest planet in our solar system? It is 142,984 kilometers in diameter and 779 million kilometers from the Sun. It has a surface temperature of -110 degrees Celsius. One year is 4,331 days long. One day lasts for 9 hours and 54 minutes.

Uranus is another big planet. It is 51,118 kilometers in diameter. It is 2,873 million kilometers from the Sun and has a temperature of -195 degrees Celsius. One year is 30,589 days long. A day lasts for 17 hours and 12 minutes.